Shrinking Violets
& Towering Tiger Lilies:
A Bouquet of Female Delights

Seven Brief Plays About Women in Distress

by Tina Howe

A SAMUEL FRENCH ACTING EDITION

NEW YORK HOLLYWOOD LONDON TORONTO

SAMUELFRENCH.COM

Copyright © 2009 by Tina Howe

ALL RIGHTS RESERVED

CAUTION: Professionals and amateurs are hereby warned that *SHRINKING VIOLETS AND TOWERING TIGER LILIES: A BOUQUET OF FEMALE DELIGHTS* is subject to a Licensing Fee. It is fully protected under the copyright laws of the United States of America, the British Commonwealth, including Canada, and all other countries of the Copyright Union. All rights, including professional, amateur, motion picture, recitation, lecturing, public reading, radio broadcasting, television and the rights of translation into foreign languages are strictly reserved. In its present form the play is dedicated to the reading public only.

The amateur live stage performance rights to *SHRINKING VIOLETS AND TOWERING TIGER LILIES: A BOUQUET OF FEMALE DELIGHTS* are controlled exclusively by Samuel French, Inc., and licensing arrangements and performance licenses must be secured well in advance of presentation. PLEASE NOTE that amateur Licensing Fees are set upon application in accordance with your producing circumstances. When applying for a licensing quotation and a performance license please give us the number of performances intended, dates of production, your seating capacity and admission fee. Licensing Fees are payable one week before the opening performance of the play to Samuel French, Inc., at 45 W. 25th Street, New York, NY 10010.

Licensing Fee of the required amount must be paid whether the play is presented for charity or gain and whether or not admission is charged.

Stock licensing fees quoted upon application to Samuel French, Inc.

For all other rights than those stipulated above, apply to: International Creative Management, 825 Eighth Avenue, New York, NY 10019, Attn: Thomas Pearson.

Particular emphasis is laid on the question of amateur or professional readings, permission and terms for which must be secured in writing from Samuel French, Inc.

Copying from this book in whole or in part is strictly forbidden by law, and the right of performance is not transferable.

Whenever the play is produced the following notice must appear on all programs, printing and advertising for the play: "Produced by special arrangement with Samuel French, Inc."

Due authorship credit must be given on all programs, printing and advertising for the play.

ISBN 978-0-573-69676-3

No one shall commit or authorize any act or omission by which the copyright of, or the right to copyright, this play may be impaired.

No one shall make any changes in this play for the purpose of production.

Publication of this play does not imply availability for performance. Both amateurs and professionals considering a production are strongly advised in their own interests to apply to Samuel French, Inc., for written permission before starting rehearsals, advertising, or booking a theatre.

No part of this book may be reproduced, stored in a retrieval system, or transmitted in any form, by any means, now known or yet to be invented, including mechanical, electronic, photocopying, recording, videotaping, or otherwise, without the prior written permission of the publisher.

IMPORTANT BILLING AND CREDIT REQUIREMENTS

All producers of *SHRINKING VIOLETS AND TOWERING TIGER LILIES: A BOUQUET OF FEMALE DELIGHTS must* give credit to the Author of the Play in all programs distributed in connection with performances of the Play, and in all instances in which the title of the Play appears for the purposes of advertising, publicizing or otherwise exploiting the Play and/or a production. The name of the Author *must* appear on a separate line on which no other name appears, immediately following the title and *must* appear in size of type not less than fifty percent of the size of the title type.

APPEARANCES, premiered in 1982 as part of Ensemble Studio Theatre's Marathon of short plays. The production was directed by Douglas Johnson

GRACE	Jane Hoffman
IVY	Wende Dasteel

THE DIVINE FALLACY was originally commissioned by The Actors Theatre of Louisville, 2000. The production was directed by Jon Jory with the following cast:

VICTOR	Tom Nelis
DOROTHY	Woodwyn Koons

WATER MUSIC premiered in 2003 as part of Ensemble Studio Theatre's Marathon of short plays. The production was directed by Pam MacKinnon with the following cast:

ROZ	Lizbeth Mackay
JESUS	Juan Carlos Hernandez
OPHELIA	Laura Heisler

THROUGH A GLASS DARKLY was commissioned by the Atlantic Theater Company, 2006. The production was directed by Christian Parker, with the following cast:

DR. CHEKHOV	Geoffrey Nauffts
KITTY	Kate Blumberg

SKIN DEEP premiered as part of the 2007 Summer Shorts Series, at 59E59. The production was directed by Laura Barnett with the following cast

DR. JOEL MARVELL, A DERMATOLOGIST	Grant Shaud
DAPHNE, A NYMPH	James Katherine Flynn
APOLLO, A GOD	Joe Kolbow

MILK AND WATER was commissioned by the University of Maryland, Baltimore County, for the their third Annual 10-Minute Play Festival, 2008. The production was directed by Lynn Watson with the following cast:

RO	Renata Melillo
CANADA	Tanika Cook
JOAN	Samantha Duvall
APRIL	Ellen Line
MAGDA	Katie Anson
WHAT'S HER NAME	Cristina Mangum

INTRODUCTION

You'd think a ten minute play would be a miniature full length play, the way toy poodles are just smaller versions of the standard variety, but on the contrary! Because time is so compressed, these miniatures need wings instead of paws. They're not chips off the old block, but mutants who can speak, sing and breathe under water! They have to have special powers if they're going to jump through all their hoops in ten minutes.

My toy poodles tend to be women, since mutating comes so easily to them. See how quickly Ovid's nymphs transform into cows, trees and starry nights as they flee from the pursuing gods. One minute they're human and the next, a lowing heifer. So whenever I write a ten minute play I put a damsel in serious distress. The tighter the ropes that bind her to the railroad tracks the better. That way ultra fancy footwork is called for. Hence the title of this collection: "Shrinking Violets and Towering Tiger Lilies." My frightened violets become ferocious tiger lilies. They're one and the same – brilliant quick change artists.

So, what happened to the toy poodles, you ask?

See that? They turned into flowers right before your eyes – presented in order in which they bloomed!

-Tina Howe

TABLE OF CONTENTS

Appearances 9
Teeth 27
The Divine Fallacy 37
Water Music 47
Through a Glass Darkly 59
Skin Deep 71
Milk and Water 81

APPEARANCES

CHARACTERS

GRACE MATTHEWS – The woman who guards the fitting room, 50s
IVY WALL – A panic stricken shopper, 30s

SETTING

Three areas of a ladies' fitting room in a cut rate department store: the desk out front with its attendant rack of discarded clothing, rows of dressing rooms off to one side and the interior of one of the rooms.

(*AT RISE:* **GRACE** *is sitting at her desk next to the discard rack, reading a trashy paperback novel. The joyous soprano-alto duet, "Jesu Der Meine Seele" from Bach's Cantata #78 plays. Nothing happens for several moments, then* **IVY**, *dressed in a bulky winter coat, comes staggering up to her with 20 dresses falling out of her arms.*)

GRACE. Just one moment! You can't bring all of those in here!

IVY. *(dropping them left and right)* Oooooooops!

GRACE. You're only allowed to try on six items at a time.

IVY. *(trying to scoop them up)* I'm sorry, I'm sorry…

GRACE. Miss! Did you hear me?

IVY. They keep falling off the hangers…

GRACE. You'll have to leave some of them with me.

IVY. *(Having finally gathered everything up into a huge ball, loses her balance and flings everything on* **GRACE***'s desk, including herself.)* WHOOOOOPS!!!

GRACE. HEY! WHAT DO YOU THINK YOU'RE DOING?

IVY. *(laughing with embarrassment as she struggles to get organized)* I lost my balance…I was just trying to…Oh God, I'm sorry, I'm sorry…

GRACE. How many items do you have there anyway?

IVY. Let's see: 1,2,3,4,5,6,7,8…*(She starts teetering under her load.)*

GRACE. *(rising to protect her desk)* OH, NO YOU DON'T…

(**IVY** *lurches into the first dressing room she sees. There's a loud crash.*)

GRACE. HEY, COME BACK HERE! I DIDN'T ASSIGN YOU THAT ROOM!

IVY. *(from offstage)* WHOOPS…! OH NO, DID I DO THAT? *(assorted screams, thuds and mewing sounds)* I'm sorry, I'm sorry, I'm sorry…

(an ominous silence)

IVY. *(lurching back into view, dropping dresses every which way)* Hi, I'm back.

GRACE. The customers don't select their dressing rooms, *I* do! How do you expect me to keep track of the merchandise unless I know how many items pass through here? *(She unwittingly stands on one of the dresses.)*

IVY. Excuse me, I'm afraid you're…uh…I'm sorry…if you could you just…

GRACE. *(not budging, oblivious)* There are rules customers have to follow, I don't care *who* they are! Eleanor Roosevelt, Amelia Earhart Greta Garbo…

IVY. *(dropping to her hands and knees, trying to move her)* Move your foot an inch to one side…not even an inch, just a smidgen…

GRACE. Or Little Red Riding Hood!

IVY. Thaaaat's it…just a tad over this way…Gently, gently…

GRACE. First, you have to let me count the number of items you want to try on, and second, you have to wait for me to assign you a room. *(stepping on another part of the dress)*

IVY. Almost, almost…

GRACE. Running this place isn't as easy as it looks! Thousands of dollars worth of merchandise pass through here every day.

IVY. Just a bit to the left…

GRACE. The customers would steal you blind if given half a chance! *(stepping off the dress)*

IVY. *(snatching it up)* Thank you very much!

GRACE. I once caught a woman trying to sneak the carpet off the floor. That's right, over 35 yards of wall to wall carpeting! Here, give me those…Let's go back to my desk so I can count them all.

(**IVY** *scoops up the rest of the dresses and follows* **GRACE** *to her desk.*)

GRACE. *(hanging them on the reject rack)* God's truth! She brought this enormous canvas fold up bag with her. I told her she'd have to check it at the desk. "Oh no!" she says. "I've got all my try-on blouses in here, plus some extra pairs of shoes. I always bring this bag with me." So like an idiot, I tell her it's OK. Just this once, and the next thing I know, my desk and chair start sliding down the hall. So I go charging into her dressing room and there she is, on her hands and knees, prying up the edges of the carpet with a crow bar and stuffing it into her bag. I couldn't believe my eyes…How she thought she could just tiptoe out of here with 35 yards of wall-to-wall carpeting trailing behind her…

IVY. Our annual office party is tonight and I want to stand out. *(revealing a hopeless dress under her coat)* I thought this dress would be perfect, but when I looked in the mirror in the ladies room, I realized it was too mousy.

GRACE. *(has finally got all the dresses hung up)* OK, let's see what you've got here. *(counting them out)* 1,2,3,4,5,6,7, 8,9,10,11,12,13,14,15,16,17,18,19… God in heaven, you've brought all the merchandise in the store back here!

IVY. *(breathless)* Alex London will be there.

GRACE. *(pulling out a sexy bra)* What's this?

IVY. He's our new managing editor.

GRACE. How did a bra get in here?

IVY. You know how some people send off a kind of… *animal thing?*

GRACE. Lingerie is on the third floor!

IVY. How they make you feel they don't have any clothes on, so you're afraid to look at them for fear you'll catch a glimpse of something you're not supposed to…you know…*see!*

GRACE. Do you have things from other floors in here? *(holding up a feathered negligee)* What's *this?*

IVY. Of course they *do* have clothes on, they just have this way of suggesting that maybe...well...there's something they'd like to show you...

GRACE. *(reading the tag)* Department 215? Department 215 is down in the basement! Did you bring these up all the way from the basement?

IVY. *(increasingly flustered)* And then you start worrying something's peeking out on *you* too, but you're afraid to look for fear everything will fall off and you'll *both* be standing there, stark naked...And then you think you're losing your mind because everyone else is fully dressed, hunched over their computers, writing emails and answering telephones.

GRACE. OK, which six things do you want to try on first?

IVY. *(glancing at her watch)* Oh dear, I don't have much time. I've got to be back by 4:00 to help set up. You see, I never planned to go shopping in the first place. I just kind of...snuck out.

GRACE. After you finish trying on the first six, just come back for the next six, and so on until you find the one you want.

IVY. *(looking at them all)* Which should I try on first?

GRACE. The ones you like best. But no more than six.

IVY. It's so hard to choose.

GRACE. *(counting off the first six and handing them to her)* 1,2,3,4,5,6!

IVY. *(heading for the first dressing room)* Oh thank you, thank you so much!

GRACE. HOLD YOUR HORSES, I HAVEN'T GIVEN YOU YOUR NUMBER YET!

IVY. *(returning)* Sorry, sorry...

GRACE. *(handing her a plastic thingy with a number 6 on it)* Here you go, take any room you like.

(IVY hurtles into the first room through a tightly sprung, waist-high swinging door. She aims at hooks which she thinks are there, but aren't so everything falls on the

floor which is littered with broken hangers, torn off labels and assorted female detritus. A listing three-way mirror stands in the corner.)

IVY. HEY, THERE ARE NO HOOKS IN HERE! WHERE WILL I PUT EVERYTHING?

GRACE. On the stool.

IVY. *What* stool? There isn't any stool!

GRACE. Then it must have been stolen. You're lucky if you've still got a mirror in there. *(pause)* You *do* have a mirror, don't you?

IVY. Wait, here's a little stub of hook left. *(She gingerly hangs up her selection, then takes off her coat, looking for a place to put it.)* COULD I BRING IN A STOOL FROM ONE OF THE OTHER DRESSING ROOMS? I HAVE NO PLACE TO PUT MY COAT.

GRACE. I'm sorry, but you're not allowed to move furniture from one room to another.

*(**IVY** throws her coat over the mirror, completely obscuring it, then she takes off her dress and places it on top of her coat. She looks at her selection, picks out a grim long-sleeved, grey turtle neck number, puts it on in front of the mirror, but can't see herself, so she takes off her coat and dress, slings them over the cantilevered door and starts posing in the grey dress. It's not a success. She strikes deliberately ugly poses, then takes it off and reaches for the next one – a ghastly bright red whorish number. She puts it on, eyes closed, spreads out her arms like a diva and then opens her eyes. More outlandish poses. She finally whips it off. Dress number three is identical to the first grey dress, but much bigger)*

IVY. *(trying it on)* What's this? I thought I already tried it on! *(She looks at the ticket.)* Ohh, it's the same one in a bigger size!

(It's so big, it makes her laugh. She starts playing with it, pulling her arms and head down into the bulk of it so nothing shows except her legs, etc., etc. She finally takes

it off and mimes beating it to death. Next comes dress number 4 which is so small she can't get it over her hips. Dress number 5 has an enormous stain over the crotch, so she grabs dress number six, a crazy print that's interesting in a peculiar sort of way, but she can't reach the zipper.)

IVY. *(flinging her arms this way and that)* Ugh! I can't reach the damn zipper...Gently, gently...take it easy...almost...almost...DAMN! I almost had it...Relax...It's not going anywhere...just...sneak up on it...Ugh! Ugh! Ugh! Ugh!

GRACE. What's going on in there?

IVY. *(more and more frustrated)* I CAN'T REACH THE DAMNED ZIPPER! *(making one more frantic attempt)* Maybe if I just *fling* my arm back...Ugh, ugh, ugh, ugh!

GRACE. Come out and I'll give you a hand.

IVY. *(making one last desperate attempt, almost dislocating her shoulder)* AAAIEEEEEEEEE!

GRACE. LET ME HELP!

*(Arms wrapped around herself, **IVY** tries to lurch through the cantilevered door, but it won't open since her coat and two dresses are in the way. She finally lowers her head and comes charging out like a bull.)*

GRACE. *(catching her in her arms)* ATTA GIRL!

IVY. I can't reach it! I just...

GRACE. *(turning her around)* Well, no wonder, the zipper pull's broken off! This dress is defective! You'll have to go back out front and look for another one.

IVY. It's broken?

GRACE. That is, if there *is* another one. I don't recall one.

IVY. Just my luck, a broken zipper! And it was my favorite one.

GRACE. Honey, I'm not selling you damaged merchandise.

IVY. I don't mind, I'll use a safety pin for the time being.

GRACE. *(taking the dress off her and hanging it on the reject rack)* I'm sorry, but you can't have this dress! How were the others you tried?

IVY. Terrible!

GRACE. Well, if you want this one so badly, see if you can find another one out front.

*(**IVY** walks out of the fitting room in her slip. Several moments pass.)*

GRACE. *(rising from her desk)* HEY, WAIT A MINUTE, YOU CAN'T GO OUT THERE IN YOUR SLIP!

(more moments pass)

IVY. *(comes careening back in, hands covering her crotch and chest)* Oh. My. God! I was only in my slip! What if somebody from the office had seen me. What if Alex London had seen me? *(She tears back into her dressing room as…)*

GRACE. Boy, will I be glad when this week is over. My daughter's getting married on Saturday and it's not going to be your average intimate family wedding with a few friends. Try and guess how many people are coming? 200? 250? 300? 350? Try 450! That's right, 450 strong!

IVY. *(returning to **GRACE**'s desk, wearing her coat over her slip, hangs her first six dresses on the reject rack)* I'm back. I can't believe what I just did. *(She starts looking through the clothes on the reject rack.)*

GRACE. My future son-in-law works for the mayor. He's one of his chief speech writers and a very bright boy. Everyone's crazy about him. All of City Hall is coming and half of the Albany legislature. *(noticing **IVY**)* No honey, those are items other customers have rejected.

IVY. *(pulling out a dress)* Gee, this one's nice.

GRACE. But it's not yours.

IVY. *(holding it up to herself)* It's a great color.

GRACE. But it's not your size! Let me give you some advice.

IVY. *(pulling out another one)* OH, LOOK AT THIS ONE!

GRACE. Honey, honey...?

IVY. *(holding it up to herself and sashaying around in it)* THIS IS THE ONE!

GRACE. Forget the dress with the broken zipper, stop looking through things you didn't pick out, and try on the rest of your selection!

IVY. Really?

GRACE. Really! You'll save yourself a lot of time. *(counting out the next six dresses and handing them to her)* Here you go...1,2,3,4,5,6.

*(**IVY** returns to her dressing room and tries to hang the next batch on the hook remnant, but everything falls to the floor. She scoops it all up and slings it over the door, takes off her coat and grabs the first dress – a white polyester number with bell sleeves and a full skirt. She puts it on, grabs her purse, searching for her comb and lipstick and fluffs herself up. She looks good. She eyes herself from several angles, doing little dance steps, looking remarkably like a bride. As...)*

GRACE. You ought to see my Donna's dress – straight out of a fairy tale! Miles and miles of taffeta, ruffles at the shoulder, a whisper of seed pearls on the bodice and a train that goes for miles. *Miles!* When she tried it on, my heart stopped. I thought I'd have to be rushed to the hospital! Donna's a very pretty girl to begin with, but in that dress, with that hour class figure of hers, she was beyond beyond! Even the saleslady had a cardiac episode! Word spread and soon flocks of other brides were crowding in our fitting room for a look. It was pandemonium. They *all* wanted that dress, but Donna got it first, and it was one of a kind! *(as...)*

*(**IVY** stops admiring herself and reaches for the next dress, which is identical to the one she's wearing, but red. She holds it up, whips off the white one, slings it over the door and puts on the red, going through the same primping and posing ritual as before...As...)*

GRACE. Of course Kenny's no slouch in the looks department either – he's as handsome as the day is long – a real matinee idol. You know, the tall, dark and handsome type, with a moustache! He's been after Donna for years. He comes from a nice family. Simple people, hard working. He's one of 11. Can you imagine having 11 kids? I could no more deal with 11 kids than fly to the moon. It was all I could do to raise Donna, but to have 10 more as well...All those lives to worry about, I'd be a nervous wreck! I don't know how Kenny's mother does it. The woman's a saint, an utter saint! You see, they also have some medical problems, though they're much more serious than "problems", they're more like...disabilities...severe disabilities. It's so tragic. They're such a darling family, and then to have all that...that... *(as...)*

*(**IVY**'s agony of choosing the right dress begins. She lurches up to the mirror in the red one, does a few flirty steps, then backs up holding the white one over it, does more flirty steps – back and forth like a yo-yo gone berserk, until she finally takes off the red one and puts on the white.)*

GRACE. One of Kenny's sisters was born without legs and another only has one arm. I couldn't handle that. Having handicapped children who break your heart every time you look at them, no thank you! But Kenny's family is wonderful with them, treats them as natural as you please. You can guess who the star attractions of that wedding are going to be in their matching flower girl dresses and little white gloves. Kenny adores those girls and takes them everywhere with him, he even brings them down to the Mayor's office. The Mayor's crazy about them too, has their pictures up on his desk, right alongside photos of his own kids. Says they're an inspiration to the entire human race... *(as...)*

*(In a burst of inspiration, **IVY** puts the red dress on over the white one and starts flipping the skirts up and down)*

GRACE. Bethy, the one without legs, has these prosthetic legs that she hooks onto herself. They're amazing they're so life-like, the exact same color as her skin. The thing that really gets me about her though, and I'm probably a little strange to notice it, is every day she puts on a fresh pair of socks. That's right…Each night she discards the pair she'd been wearing and selects a clean pair for the next day. If you stop to think about it, you realize there's no way they get dirty, since she doesn't have any feet to get them all sweated up. She's just a stickler for appearances and insists on fresh socks every day, because fresh socks look better than wilted ones. Well, when I see those spanking white socks hugging those little plastic ankles of her, the cuffs folded just so, it brings tears to my eyes! That Bethy takes pride in how she looks! She knows she's been born with a handicap, but she doesn't let it get to her! And active? She does everything any normal 10 year old would do: run, jump, play sports. And sense of humor? She's a real mimic that one! You ought to hear her imitate the pop singers. *(She imitates Bethy imitating them. As…)*

IVY. *(crazier and crazier with indecision, flipping her dresses back and forth)* I CAN'T DECIDE!

GRACE. Though to be honest, I'm nervous as a witch about Donna having normal kids with Kenny. I mean, two of his sisters have missing limbs and there's one child no one's ever seen! You can't turn your back on these things. Kenny's gene pool is a disaster! Donna's very anxious about it, but refuses to talk about it. "It's between Kenny and me!", she says. "I love him and I want to have his children. They'll be all right. I know they'll be all right. It's in God's hands." Though to tell you the truth, I haven't slept a wink since the invitations went out. It's too late to call it off now. Four hundred and fifty friends are rooting for them and the decorators have already turned Gracie Mansion into a pink and white valentine. What will happen will happen, though if Donna has an armless or legless baby I don't know what I'll do. I couldn't take it, but then I'd have to take it, wouldn't I? Put on a brave face, like Bethy changing her socks every day. People adjust. I just don't know if I have it in me. I'm very weak on courage and always have been. I can't even help a blind person cross the street! As soon as I see one coming with their tapping stick, I start to panic and try to disappear, hoping to God they can't really see me. It's a terrible failing, I wish I could change. It's my most fervent prayer, "Please God, make me more accepting!"

IVY. *(bursting out of her dressing room and rushing up to* **GRACE***)* HELP ME, I CAN'T DECIDE!

GRACE. Oh, I like that on you, it's very nice!

IVY. But what about *this* one? *(She lifts up the red dress to reveal the white one.)*

GRACE. You're wearing two dresses at the same time?

IVY. *(sashaying around in the white one)* I'm going crazy!

GRACE. I've never seen anyone wear two dresses at...

IVY. What do you think? This one? Or *this*? *(dropping the red back down over the white)*

GRACE. I hope you weren't thinking about sneaking out of here in one of those.

IVY. The red brings out my color more, but there's something magical about the white one.

GRACE. *(flipping the skirts up and down)* It's amazing, no one would ever know!

IVY. What do you think? Be honest now, it's my only chance to catch his eye. If he could just... *notice* me for ten seconds... *(whirling around in the red)*

GRACE. That *is* nice, it gives you a flush!

*(***IVY** *quickly flips it over her head, whirling in the white.)*

GRACE. But then there *is* something other wordly about this one. It's a question of which he'd respond to more – innocence...

(**IVY** *switches back to the red.*)

GRACE. Or seduction...You can't have both at the same time

(**IVY** *launches into an extraordinary flamenco-type dance in which she's all innocence in white, then a smoldering temptress in red. She whips her skirts faster and faster, stomping her feet and tossing her head with appropriate yelps and mews.* **GRACE** *is speechless. Soon she's clapping and yelping herself.* **IVY** *finishes in a burst of schizophrenic dips and bows.*)

GRACE. *(applauding wildly)* BRAVA! BRAVA! I HAD NO IDEA YOU COULD DANCE LIKE THAT! YOU WERE SENSATIONAL!

IVY. *(out of breath)* Thank you, thank you...

GRACE. I MEAN, *REALLY* SENSATIONAL!

IVY. You're too kind.

GRACE. YOU COULD BE ON THE STAGE!

IVY. I don't know what came over me.

GRACE. If you do *that* at your party, you'll start a riot.

IVY. *(glancing at her watch)* Oh no, look at the time! I was supposed to be back at the office ten minutes ago. I promised Panda Schultz I'd help set up the appetizers. *(She starts taking off the red dress.)*

GRACE. Here, let me help you.

IVY. The party starts at 6:30 sharp. Panda and I have to get the appetizers ready and out by 6:15! The whole place is in an uproar because this is our first office party since Alex London joined the firm and everyone is crazy about him, men as well as women! When he walks into a room, secretaries collapse and senior editors walk into glass partitions. It's ridiculous! We're like a bunch of hysterical teenagers. You see, aside from his "animal thing," Alex London has the most beautiful mouth you've ever seen. The sort of mouth people jump off bridges for! You know, the kind with a very plump lower lip that's divided into two little mounds shaped sort of like rose petals...Generally speaking, he isn't that good looking – medium height with graying hair, nondescript eyes and a rather sallow complexion. He just has this phenomenal lower lip that drives everyone into a frenzy. You want to suck it, then bite it in half and ever so slowly...chew it into tiny bits.

GRACE. *(putting the two dresses over her arm)* You don't have to tell *me* about lips! Kenny has a phenomenal pair! It's all Donna can do not to tackle him to the ground whenever she sees him. It's half the reason she's marrying him, if you ask me. "Kenny's kisses, Ma. You wouldn't believe them! His lips are as succulent as melting ice cream!" It's all she talks about!

IVY. Everyone's dressing to kill. It will be impossible to be noticed.

GRACE. So, which will it be? When you're wearing them at the same time, it's impossible to get the full effect. *(holding the red one up to herself, posing, as...)*

IVY. All I'm hoping for is just two or three seconds of being *seen!* He doesn't even have to speak to me. I just want to be held in his gaze for a moment...finally see my reflection in his pupils. He's my boss, for God's sake! We speak to each other every day, but I can't seem to materialize when he looks at me! It's very scary because I feel as if I'm on fire, with my whole face in flames, so then I start worrying that maybe I'm crazy, that it's all in my mind...that *I'm* in my mind and don't really exist at all!

GRACE. If there were just *two* of you... *(She holds the white one up to herself and poses, as...)*

IVY. Sometimes when I'm thinking about him, I feel myself becoming almost radio-active. It's true! Once when I was on the cross town bus, I thought I saw him out the window and ZAAAAPPP, everything started heating up...my scalp, face, ears, hands, throat, and even my *teeth!* I shut my eyes, terrified I was starting to glow like some huge iridescent firefly and that everyone was

IVY. *(cont.)* staring at me, pointing and laughing. Ever since the party was announced, I've been having this dream, well actually, it's more like a nightmare...

GRACE. I've got it! *(shoving the white dress at her)* *I'll* wear the red and *you* wear the white!

IVY. There I am, standing next to the sushi bar, rice and soy sauce glistening all over my hands and face as Alex London inches closer, and I mean, *inches!*

GRACE. Now hold still. *(helping* IVY *into the white dress and putting on the red as...)*

IVY. I start thinking of all the clever things I'll say to him. So I practice in this low sexy voice, trying to sound like a movie star: "Yooo hooo, Alex! I'm right over here by the spicy tuna and mango rolls...My, but don't you look dashing tonight!" But as usual, he doesn't see me, so I start jumping up and down, waving my arms, yelling, "SPICY TUNA AND MANGO ROLLS!" And then suddenly he's gone and Panda is standing next to me wild-eyed and sobbing. "Have you heard?", she says. "Alex London has left the firm. He cleared out of his office this morning and no one has seen him since!" The place is in an uproar with secretaries throwing themselves into punch bowls, research assistants slashing their wrists with chopsticks, broken glass everywhere... And then it's around two in the morning... Everyone's gone home and I'm at my desk typing – tappity tap, tap – when I start noticing something strange about the keys...They feel oddly soft and moist...I look down and instead of seeing the lettered tabs, there are all these...tiny mouths...about 30 or 40 of them, and they're all Alex London's mouth! I'm so surprised, I try to pull my hands away, but they won't let go. They clamp their little lips around my fingers and hold on for dear life. It feels so strange, because there are so many of them and they're so small, like darting tropical fish. "Alex, is that you?" I ask. "Are you hiding in my computer?" But of course he doesn't answer. There's just this...light smacking, popping sound...My initial surprise gives way to delight as they swarm around my fingers, nibbling and sucking. Their lips are so soft and their tongues so incredibly warm… It's hard to describe because it sounds rather disgusting, when in fact, it was really rather… *nice!*

GRACE. *(revolted)* And I thought *I* had weird dreams!

IVY. Eventually, all the mouths became this one huge mouth…glistening and pulsing, reaching for my arms, shoulders, neck and face…

GRACE. Please, no more! I get the picture!

IVY. Moonlight gushed through the window and everything started to flood and dissolve…

GRACE. *(pulling her back to the three-way mirror in her dressing room)* We've got to make our decision before the damned store closes on us!

(Arms linked, the two stand in front of the mirror.)

IVY. *(the situation finally sinking in)* OH! MY! GOD!

*(**GRACE** does a little pirouette in the red dress.)*

IVY. YOU PUT ON THE OTHER DRESS! YOU LOOK INCREDIBLE!

GRACE. *(doing a few more dance steps)* Please… It's nothing…

IVY. I just never pictured you all dolled up!

GRACE. This is my color.

IVY. WE LOOK LIKE TWINS!

*(**IVY** starts kicking like a Rockette. **GRACE** joins her.)*

GRACE. OK, honey, you've got to decide which one you'll take.

(They do a few turns examining each other.)

IVY. The white!

GRACE. The white!

IVY. Definitely the white!

GRACE. No contest!

IVY. *(hugging her)* We did it! We did it!

GRACE. Well, this is a first! I've never taken off my clothes for a customer before!

IVY. I couldn't have done it without you! *(hugging her and kissing her cheek)* Thank you so much!

GRACE. Don't mention it.

IVY. No, you saved my life! You *really* saved it!

GRACE. Well, I enjoyed it, though to be honest, I don't know what came over me...trying on the merchandise during store hours.

IVY. If Alex London doesn't notice me tonight...

GRACE. Oh, he'll notice you alright! All you needed was the right attitude!

IVY. *(spinning and laughing)* Look at me!

GRACE. It's like Bethy, she wasn't born with legs, so she goes out and *finds* herself a pair!

IVY. Just...look at me!

GRACE. She doesn't just lie around in some grocery cart waiting for someone to push her, she hauls herself over to the hospital and *gets* a pair of legs with cute little feet to match!

IVY. *(pulling the two sides of the mirror in on herself, sending out shards of light)* I'M BEAUTIFUL! REALLY... BEAUTIFUL! COME ON, JOIN ME! *(pulling **GRACE** into the mirror with her)*

GRACE. When you stop to think about it, we're all hanging on for dear life. This one's got no legs, that one's hidden out back, I'm going deaf in one ear, you have trouble materializing...The whole thing is to keep going! Forget the high altitude and don't look down!

IVY. *(The light around them intensifies.)* SPIN, WOMAN SPIN! WE LOOK LIKE SOMETHING OUT OF A RENAISSANCE PAINTING! LOOK, AT US! JUST...LOOK!

*(The soprano-alto duet returns as **IVY** and **GRACE** spin, radiating with the wattage of a thousand angels.)*

End of Play

TEETH

CHARACTERS

DR. ROSE – A dentist, 40s–50s
AMY – His patient, 20s–40s
VOICE OF RADIO ANNOUNCER

SETTING

A modest one-man dentist's office in midtown Manhattan. An FM radio is tuned to a classical music station. It's March 21, Johann Sebastian Bach's birthday, and we hear the rollicking Presto from his Toccata in C minor.

(AT RISE: The whine of a high-powered dentist's drill slowly asserts itself. In blackout…)

DR. ROSE. Still with me…?

AMY. *(garbled because his hands are in her mouth)* Aaargh…

DR. ROSE. *(hums along as the drilling gets louder)* You've heard his Goldberg reissue, haven't you?

AMY. Aaargh…

DR. ROSE. *(groans with pleasure)* Unbelievable!

(The drilling gets ferocious.)

AMY. *Ow…ow!*

DR. ROSE. Whoops, sorry about that. Okay, you can rinse.

*(Lights up on **AMY** lying prone in a dentist's chair with a bib around her neck. She sits up, takes a swig of water, sloshes it around in her mouth, and spits it emphatically into the little bowl next to her. She flops back down, wiping her mouth.)*

DR. ROSE. Glenn Gould. Glenn Gould is the penultimate Bach keyboard artist of our time, period! Open, please. *(He resumes drilling.)* No one else can touch him!

AMY. Aarg…

DR. ROSE. Wanda Landowska, Roselyn Turek, Trevor Pinnock…forget it!

AMY. Aarg…

DR. ROSE. *(drilling with rising intensity.)* Andras Schiff, Igor Kipness, Anthony Newman…no contest!

AMY. Aarg…

DR. ROSE. Listen to the man…! The elegance of his phrasing, the clarity of his touch….The joy! The joy! *(He roars.)*

AMY. *(practically jumping out of her seat)* OOOOOWWWWWWW!

DR. ROSE. Sorry, sorry, afraid I slipped. *(His drilling returns to normal.)* Hear how he hums along in a different key? The man can't contain himself…. *(He roars again, calms down for a spate of drilling, idly starts humming along with the music.)* You know, you're my third patient… no, make that fourth…that's pulled out a filling with candy this week. What was the culprit again?

AMY. *(garbled)* Bit O'Honey.

DR. ROSE. Almond Roca…?

AMY. *(garbled.)* Bit O'Honey.

DR. ROSE. Jujubes?

AMY. *(less garbled.)* Bit O'Honey, Bit O'Honey!

DR. ROSE. Yup, saltwater taffy will do it every time! Okay, Amy, the worst is over. You can rinse. *(He hangs up the drill.)*

(AMY rinses and spits with even more fury.)

DR. ROSE. Hey, hey, don't break my bowl on me! *(fussing with his tools.)* Now, where did I put that probe…? I can't seem to hold onto anything these days….

(AMY flops back down with a sigh.)

DR. ROSE. *(in a little singsong.)* Where are you?…Where are you…? Ahhhhh, here it is! Okay…let's just take one last look before we fill you up. Open. *(He disappears into her mouth with the probe.)* Amy, Amy, you're still grinding your teeth at night, aren't you!

AMY. *(anguished)* Aaaaarrrrhhh!

DR. ROSE. You've got to wear that rubber guard I gave you.

AMY. *(completely garbled.)* But I can't breathe when it's on!

AMY. *(incomprehensible)* I feel like I'm choking! I've tried to wear it, I really have, but I always wake up gasping for air. See, I can't breathe through my nose. If I could breathe through my nose, it wouldn't be a problem….

DR. ROSE. I know they take getting used to, but you're doing irreparable damage to your supporting bone layer, and once that goes… *(He whistles her fate.)*

*(A **RADIO ANNOUNCER** has come on in the background during this.)*

RADIO ANNOUNCER. That was Glenn Gould playing Bach's Toccata in C minor, BWV listing 911. And to continue with our birthday tribute to J. S. Bach, we now turn to his Cantata BWV 80, "Ein Feste"Burg," as performed by the English Chamber Orchestra under the direction of Raymond Leppard.

(The music begins.)

DR. ROSE. *(comes out of her mouth.)* Well, let's whip up a temporary filling and get you out of here. *(He rummages through his tray of tools.)*

AMY. Dr. Rose, could I ask you something?

DR. ROSE. Of course, today's March twenty-first, Bach's birthday! *(Some instruments fall; he quickly recovers them.)* Whoops…

AMY. I keep having this recurring nightmare.

DR. ROSE. Oh, I love this piece. I used to sing it in college. Mind if I turn it up?

AMY. I just wonder if you've heard it before.

DR. ROSE. *(Turns up the volume, singing along, as he returns to his tray and starts sorting out his things, which keep dropping. He quickly retrieves them, never stopping his singing.)*
Ein feste Burg ist unser Gott,
Ein gute Wehr und Waffen….whoops.
Er hilft uns frei aus aller, Not,
Die uns itzt hat…whoops…betroffen."

AMY. I have it at least three times a week now.

DR. ROSE. I came this close to being a music major. This close!

AMY. I wake up exhausted with my whole jaw throbbing. Waa…waa…waa!

DR. ROSE. Okay, let's just open this little bottle of cement here. *(He starts struggling with the lid.)*

AMY. You know, the old... *teeth-granulating-on-you* dream! *(She stifles a sob.)* You're at a party flashing a perfect smile when suddenly you hear this splintering sound like someone smashing teacups in the next room.... ping...tock...crackkkkkkkkkk...tinkle, tinkle. "Well, someone's having a good time!" you say to yourself, expecting to see some maniac swinging a sledgehammer....

(Having a worse and worse time with the bottle, **DR. ROSE** *moves behind her chair so she can't see him.)*

DR. ROSE. Ugh...ugh...ugh...ugh...ugh!

AMY. So you casually look around, and of course there *is* no maniac...! Then you feel these prickly shards clinging to your lips.... You try and brush them away, but suddenly your mouth is filled with them. You can't spit them out fast enough! *(She tries.)*

DR. ROSE. Goddamnit! *(He goes through a series of silent contortions trying to open it – behind his back, up over his head, down between his legs, etc. etc.)*

AMY. *(still spitting and wiping)* People are starting to stare.... You try to save face. *(to the imagined partygoers)* "Well, what do you know.... I seem to have taken a bite out of my coffee cup! Silly me!" *(She laughs, frantically wiping.)*

DR. ROSE. Goddamn son of a bitch, what's going on here?

AMY. That's what I want to know!

DR. ROSE. Is this some kind of conspiracy or what?

AMY. Why me? What did I do?

DR. ROSE. They must weld these tops on.

AMY. Then I catch a glimpse of myself in the mirror...

DR. ROSE. *(starting to cackle.)* Think you can outsmart me...? *(He starts whacking a heavy tool down on the lid.)*

AMY. You got it! My teeth are spilling out of my mouth in little pieces. I frantically try and smoosh them back in, but they have nothing to hold on to. Then they start granulating on me...fsssssssssssssssss...It's like trying to build a sand castle inside an hourglass!

(**DR. ROSE** *is having a worse and worse time. He finally sits on the floor, banging the bottle down as hard as he can.*)

AMY. My mouth is a blaze of gums. We are talking pink for *miles*...! Magellan staring out over the Pacific Ocean during a sunset in 1520 – *(as Magellan)* "Pink...pink... pink...pink!"

(**DR. ROSE** *starts to whimper as he pounds.*)

AMY. What does it *mean*, is what I'd like to know! I mean, teeth are supposed to last forever, right? They hold up through floods, fires, earthquakes, and wars...the one part of us that endures.

DR. ROSE. Open, damnit. Open, damnit, Open, damnit....

AMY. So if they granulate on you, where does that leave you? *Nowhere!*

DR. ROSE. *(curling up into the fetal position and focusing on smaller moves in a tiny voice)* Come on...come on... Please? Pretty please?·Pretty, lovely, ravishing please?

AMY. You could have been rain or wind, for all anybody knows. That's pretty scary...*(starting to get weepy)* One minute you're laughing at a party and the next you've evaporated into thin air...*(putting on a voice)* "Remember Amy? Gee, I wonder whatever happened to her?" *(in another voice)* "Gosh, it's suddenly gotten awfully chilly in here. Where's that *wind* coming from?" *(teary again)* I mean, we're not around for that long as it is, so then to suddenly...I'm sorry, I'm sorry. It's just I have this um...long-standing...Oh, God, here we go ... *(starting to break down)* Control yourself! Control... control!

(**DR. ROSE** *is now rolled up in a ball beyond speech. He clutches the bottle, whimpering and emitting strange little sobs.*)

AMY. See, I have this long-standing um...fear of death? It's something you're born with. I used to sob in my father's arms when I was only...Oh, boy! See, once you start thinking about it, I mean...*really* thinking about it...You know, time going on for ever and ever and ever and ever and you're not there...It can get pretty scary...! We're not talking missing out on a few measly centuries here, but all...time! You know, dinosaurs, camel trains, holy wars, boom! and back to dinosaurs again? *(more and more weepy)* Eternity!...Dinosaurs, camel trains, holy wars, boom! Dinosaurs, camel trains, holy wars, boom!...Dinosaurs, camel trains, holy wars....Stop it, Amy...just...*stop it!*

DR. ROSE. *(broken)* I can't open this bottle.

AMY. *(wiping away her tears)* Dr. Rose! What are you doing down there?

DR. ROSE. I've tried everything.

AMY. What's wrong?

DR. ROSE. *(reaching the bottle up to her)* I can't open it.

AMY. *(taking it)* Here, let me try.

DR. ROSE. I'm afraid I'm having a breakdown.

AMY. I'm good at this kind of thing,

DR. ROSE. I don't know, for some time now I just haven't...

AMY. *(Puts the bottle in her mouth, clamps down on it with her back teeth and unscrews the lid with one turn. She hands it back to him.)* Here you go.

DR. ROSE. *(rises and advances toward her menacingly)* You should never...*ever do that!*

AMY. *(drawing back)* What?

DR. ROSE. Open a bottle with your teeth.

AMY. I do it all the time,

DR. ROSE. Teeth are very fragile. They're not meant to be used as tools!

AMY. Sorry, sorry,

DR. ROSE. I just don't believe the way people mistreat them. We're only given one set of permanent teeth in a lifetime, *One set and that's it!*

AMY. I won't do it again. I promise.

DR. ROSE. Species flourish and disappear, only our teeth remain. Open, please. *(He puts cotton wadding in her mouth.)* You must respect them, take care of them…. Oh, why even bother talking about it; no one ever listens to me, anyway. Wider, please. *(He puts in more cotton and a bubbling saliva drain.)* Okay, let's fill this baby and get you on your way. *(He dabs in bits of compound.)* So, how's work these days?

AMY. Aarg…

DR. ROSE. Same old rat race, huh?

AMY. Aarg…

(During this, the final chorus, "Das Wort sie sollen lassen stahn" has started to play.)

AMY. *(slightly garbled)* What is that tune? It's so familiar.

DR. ROSE. "A Mighty Fortress Is Our God."

AMY. Right, right! I used to sing it in Sunday school a hundred years ago.

DR. ROSE. Actually, Bach stole the melody from Martin Luther.

AMY. *(bursts into song, garbled, the saliva drain bubbling)* "A Mighty Fortress Is Our God…"

AMY.	**DR. ROSE.** *(joining her)*
…a bulwark never failing…	*…Und kein' Dank dazu haben,*
Our helper he amid the flood	*Er ist bei uns wehl auf dem Plan*
Of mortal ills prevailing.	*Mit seinem Geist und Gaben.*
For still our ancient foe,	*Nehmen sie uns den Leib,*
Doth seek to work us woe…	*Gut, Ehr, Kind und Weib….*

(Their voices swell louder and louder.)

End of Play

THE DIVINE FALLACY

CHARACTERS

VICTOR HUGO – a photographer, 30s–40s
DOROTHY KISS – a writer, 20s–30s

SETTING

Victor's studio in downtown Manhattan. It looks like a surreal garden blooming with white umbrellas and reflective silver screens. As the lights rise we hear the joyful bass-soprano duet, "Mit unser macht ist nichts getan," from Bach's chorale, Ein feste Burg, BWV 80.

(*AT RISE: It's a freezing day in late February.* **VICTOR**, *dressed in black, has been waiting for* **DOROTHY** *for over an hour. There's a tentative knock at his door.*)

VICTOR. Finally! *(rushing to answer it)* Dorothy Kiss?

(**DOROTHY** *steps in, glasses fogged over and very out of breath. She's a mousy woman dressed in layers of mismatched clothes. An enormous coat covers a bulky sweater which covers a gauzy white dress. A tangle of woolen scarves is wrapped around her neck*)

DOROTHY. *(rooted to the spot)* Victor Hugo?

VICTOR. At last!

DOROTHY. I'm sorry, I'm sorry, I got lost.

VICTOR. Come in.

DOROTHY. I reversed the numbers of your address.

VICTOR. We don't have much time.

DOROTHY. *(with a shrill laugh)* I went to 22 West 17th instead of 17 West 22nd!

VICTOR. I have to leave for Paris in an hour.

DOROTHY. The minute I got there, I knew something was wrong.

VICTOR. *(looking at his watch)* No, make that forty-five minutes.

DOROTHY. There were all these naked people milling around. *(pause)* With pigeons.

VICTOR. The spring collections open tomorrow.

DOROTHY. They were so beautiful.

VICTOR. It's going to be a mad house…Come in, please…

(He strides into the studio and starts setting up his equipment.)

DOROTHY. I didn't realize they came in so many colors.

DOROTHY.	VICTOR.
Red, green, yellow, purple… I think they'd been dyed.	A tidal wave of photographers is coming from all over the world.

(pause)

VICTOR. I swore last year would be my last, but a man's got to make a living, right? *(turning to look for her)* Hey, where did you go?

(**DOROTHY** *waves at him from the door.*)

VICTOR. Miss Kiss…we've got to hurry if you want me to do this.

(**DOROTHY** *makes a strangled sound.*)

VICTOR. *(guiding her into the room)* Come in, come in… I won't bite.

DOROTHY. *(with a shrill laugh)* My glasses are fogged over! I can't see a thing! *(She takes them off and wipes them with the end of one of her scarves.)*

VICTOR. Here, let me help you off with your coat.

(They go through a lurching dance as he tries to unwrap all her scarves, making her spin like a top.)

VICTOR.	DOROTHY.
Hold still… easy does It. Atta girl…	Whoops, I was just… Sorry, sorry, sorry, sorry…

(He finally succeeds. They look at each other and smile, breathing heavily.)

VICTOR. So *you're* Daphne's sister?!

DOROTHY. Dorothy Kiss, the *writer!*

(**VICTOR** *struggles to see the resemblance.*)

DOROTHY. I know. It's a shocker.

VICTOR. No, no…

DOROTHY. She's only the top fashion model in the country, and here I am…Miss Muskrat!

VICTOR. The more I look at you, the more I see the resemblance.

DOROTHY. You don't have to do that.

VICTOR. No really. There's something about your forehead...

DOROTHY. I take after my father. The rodent side of the family... Small, nondescript, close to the ground...

(She makes disturbing rodent sounds.)

VICTOR. You're funny.

DOROTHY. I try.

(silence)

VICTOR. So...

DOROTHY. *(grabbing her coat and lurching towards the door)* Goodbye, nice meeting you.

VICTOR. *(barring her way)* Hey, hey, just a minute...

DOROTHY. I can let myself out.

VICTOR. Daphne said you were coming out with a new novel and needed a photograph for the back cover.

DOROTHY. Another time...

VICTOR. It sounded wild.

DOROTHY. Oh God, oh God...

VICTOR. Something about a woman whose head keeps falling off.

DOROTHY. This was *her* idea, not mine! I hate having my picture taken! *(struggling to get past him)* I hate it, hate it, hate it, hate it, hate it, hate it, hate it, hate it...

VICTOR. *(grabbing her arm)* She told me you might react like this.

DOROTHY. *Hate it, hate it, hate it, hate it!*

VICTOR. Dorothy, Dorothy...

*(**DOROTHY** desperately tries to escape. **VICTOR** grabs her in his arms as she continues to fight him, kicking her legs. He finally plunks her down in a chair. They breathe heavily. A silence.)*

DOROTHY. Why can't you set up your camera in my brain? Bore a hole in my skull and let 'er rip. *(She makes lurid sound effects.)* There's no plainness here, but heaving oceans ringed with pearls and ancient cities rising in the mist...Grab your tripod and activate your zoom, wonders are at hand...Holy men calling the faithful to prayer as women shed their clothes at the river's edge...Click! Jeweled elephants drink beside them, their trunks shattering the surface like breaking glass. Click! Their reflections shiver and merge, woman and elephant becoming one...Slender arms dissolving into rippling tusks, loosened hair spreading into shuddering flanks...Click, click, click! Now you see them, now you don't...A breast, a tail, a winking eye...Click! Macaws scream over head *(sound effect),* or is it the laughter of the women as they drift further and further from the shore, their shouts becoming hoarse and strange...*(sound effect)* Click! *(tapping her temple)* Aim your camera here, Mr. Hugo. *This* is where beauty lies...Mysterious, inchoate and out of sight!

*(silence as **VICTOR** stares at her)*

DOROTHY. *(suddenly depressed)* I don't know about you, but I could use a drink.

VICTOR. *(as if in a dream)* Right, right...

DOROTHY. VICTOR?! *(pause)* I'd like a drink, if you don't mind!

VICTOR. Coming right up. What's your poison?

DOROTHY. Vodka, neat.

VICTOR. You got it! *(He lurches to a cabinet and fetches a bottle of vodka and a glass.)*

DOROTHY. That's alright, I don't need a glass. *(She grabs the bottle and chugs an enormous amount.)* Thanks, I needed that!

VICTOR. Holy Shit!

DOROTHY. *(wiping her mouth)* Where are my manners? I forgot about you. *(passing him the bottle)* Sorry, sorry...

VICTOR. *(pours a small amount in a glass and tips it towards her)* Cheers!

(She raises an imaginary glass.)

DOROTHY. Could I ask you a personal question?

VICTOR. Shoot.

DOROTHY. Are you really related to *the* Victor Hugo?

VICTOR. Strange but true.

DOROTHY. Really, really?

VICTOR. *Really!* He was my great great grandfather! *(bowing)* A votre service.

DOROTHY. He's my favorite writer! He's all I read… Over and over and over again! I can't believe I'm standing in the same room with you!

(She suddenly grabs one of his cameras and starts taking pictures of him.)

VICTOR. Hey, what are you doing? That's a two thousand dollar camera you're using!

(He lunges for it. She runs from him, snapping his picture.)

DOROTHY. A direct descendent of Victor Hugo…

VICTOR. *(chasing her)* Put that down!

DOROTHY. *(snapping him at crazy angles)* No one will believe this!

VICTOR. Give it here! *(finally catching her)* I SAID: GIVE ME THAT CAMERA!

(They struggle. A torrent of blood gushes from her hand.)

DOROTHY. Ow! Ow!

VICTOR. *(frozen to the spot)* Miss Kiss…Miss Kiss…Oh my God, my God…

*(**DOROTHY** gulps for air.)*

VICTOR. What did I do?

(Her breathing slowly returns to normal.)

VICTOR. Are you alright?

DOROTHY. *(weakly)* A tourniquet...I need a tourniquet.

VICTOR. On the double! *(He races around looking for one.)*

DOROTHY. Wait, my sock...*(She kicks off one of her boots and removes a white sock.)*

VICTOR. *(running to her side)* Here, let me help.

DOROTHY. No, I can do it. *(She expertly ties it to stop the flow of blood.)*

VICTOR. How are you feeling?

DOROTHY. Better thanks.

VICTOR. I'm so sorry.

DOROTHY. It's not your fault.

VICTOR. I didn't mean to hurt you.

DOROTHY. I have a stigmata.

VICTOR. *What?*

DOROTHY. I said I have a stigmata. It bleeds when I get wrought up.

VICTOR. *You have a stigmata?*

DOROTHY. Several, actually.

VICTOR. Jesus Christ!

DOROTHY. Jesus Christ, indeed.

VICTOR. A *stigmata?* In *my* studio?!

(silence)

DOROTHY. I'm afraid you're going to miss your plane to Paris. I'm sorry. *(A silence. She hands him his camera.)* Well, I guess you maight as well take my picture.

VICTOR. Right, right...your picture.

(She removes her glasses and bulky sweater and looks eerily beautiful in her white gauzy dress.)

DOROTHY. I'm as ready as I'm ever going to be.

*(**VICTOR** is stunned, unable to move.)*

DOROTHY. Yoo hoo...Mr. Hugo?

VICTOR. You're so beautiful!

DOROTHY. *(lowering her eyes)* Please!

VICTOR. You look so sad…Like an early Christian martyr.

(A great light starts to emanate from her. **VICTOR** *races to get his camera and begins taking her picture.)*

VICTOR. *(breaking down)* I can't…I can't…I just…can't.

DOROTHY. Victor, Victor, it's alright…We all have something…You have your eye, Daphne has her beauty and I have this. It's OK. It makes me who I am.

*(****VICTOR*** *struggles to control himself.)*

DOROTHY. Listen to me…Listen…When the Navahos weave a blanket, they leave in a hole to let the soul out – the flaw, the fallacy – call it what you will. It's part of the design, the most important part – faith, surrender, a mysterious tendency to bleed…

VICTOR. I'm so ashamed.

DOROTHY. You did your job. You took my picture.

VICTOR. But I didn't see you.

DOROTHY. Shh, shh…

VICTOR. I was blind.

DOROTHY. Shhhhhh…

VICTOR. *(breaking down again)* Blind, blind, blind…

*(****DOROTHY*** *rises and places her hands over his eyes and then raises them in a gesture of benediction.)*

DOROTHY. There, there, it's alright. It's over. You did it. You took my picture.

(The lights blaze around them as the closing measures of Bach's duet swell.)

End of Play

WATER MUSIC

CHARACTERS

ROZ – A high school English teacher, 50s–60s
JESUS – The sexy Latino life guard, early 30s
OPHELIA – Polonius' mad daughter from *Hamlet*, 20s

SETTING

The whirlpool at a neighborhood health club on the Upper West Side of New York City.

(*AT RISE: The rousing allegro from Suite #1 of Handel's* Water Music *plays.* **JESUS** *the lifeguard, sits by the offstage lap pool trying to stay awake. Nothing happens for several moments then* **ROZ** *makes her way over to the whirlpool, turns on the jets and sinks in with a contented sigh.*)

ROZ. *(removing her cap and goggles)* Fifteen minutes of continuous laps...Not bad.

(*She positions herself so that that one of the jets hits her lower back. She's in heaven, but then the temperature of the water starts to drop. She moves from jet to jet, trying to get warm*)

ROZ. What's going on with the temperature in here? One minute it's a toasty 103 degrees and the next I feel like I'm being blended into a frozen margarita! *(struggling to get out)* HELLLP! HELLLLLLP!

JESUS. *(waking with a start, in Spanish:)* Who? Where? What?

ROZ. *Jesus,* Jesus!

JESUS. *(rushing over to her)* Hey-zoos, my name is Hay-zoos

ROZ. *(flailing her arms)* I DON'T CARE WHAT YOUR GOD-DAMNED NAME IS, I'M LOSING ALL FEELING IN MY LEGS!

JESUS. *(helping her out)* HEY-zoos Eduardo de Los Angeles Avila Morales!

ROZ. *(moving stiffly)* Meet the Abominable Snow Woman!

JESUS. *(feeling the water)* It's not so cold!

ROZ. What do you know about cold? You're a hot blooded Latino who grew up in some steaming tropical rain forest on the outskirts of Machu Picchu!

(*A brief silence. Then* **JESUS** *brings the rain forest to life, imitating chattering monkeys and screeching parrots.*)

ROZ. Nice…very nice! But I'd be even more impressed if you took care of things around here!

JESUS. My father taught me how to converse with all of God's creatures – from the tiny glittering butterfly to the gigantic killer whale. *(more sound effects)*

ROZ. Yeah, yeah…This whirlpool is a disgrace! If it's not freezing, it's filthy! You know what I saw floating on the bottom last week? A nest of pubic hair, a half eaten strawberry and a school of albino shrimp! They were wearing mittens. That's right. Teeny tiny *red* mittens. *(barely audible)* With matching scarves…! Life is hard enough without being accosted by toxic refuse! *You* try being an English teacher in the New York City public school system for 25 years! I have bone spurs in my neck, arthritis in my knees and an asthma condition that sends me to the emergency room twice a month! I come here to get a little relief! Not to be sucked into some aberrant sewer system…If you spent less time doing laps before the club opens, you'd be more aware of what's going on in this shit hole! But no, you've got to swim just four more miles. I've never seen anyone so obsessed with swimming. Pretty soon you'll be tackling the Atlantic ocean!

JESUS. Not the Atlantic ocean, the English Channel!

ROZ. The English Channel, the Atlantic Ocean, the River Styx! What difference does it make? You're so water logged you've forgotten how to maneuver on dry land.

(There's a celestial sound. The jets shut off, the lights flicker and we hear torrents of rushing water. **OPHELIA** *suddenly rises out of the whirlpool. She's soaking wet, dressed in a clinging Elizabethan gown, covered with vines and wild flowers)*

JESUS. *(falls to his knees and starts praying in Spanish, thinking she's the Virgin Mary)* Hail Mary, full of grace, blessed art thou among women, and blessed is the fruit of thy womb Jesus, *(etc. etc. overlapping)*

(ROZ *stares at her, dumbfounded.* OPHELIA *steps out of the pool and hands her a variety of wild flowers.*)

OPHELIA. *(speaking with an English accent)* "There's rosemary, that's for remembrance; pray you love, remember: and there is pansies, that's for thoughts…"

ROZ. *Ophelia?*

OPHELIA. "There's fennel for you, and columbines: – there's rue for you; and here's some for me: – we may call it herb-grace o' Sundays…"

JESUS. *(in Spanish:)* Forgive me, Mother for I have sinned. *(He returns to his praying, overlapping* OPHELIA.*)*

ROZ. Shakespeare's Ophelia in our whirlpool!

OPHELIA. *(handing her more flowers)* "O, you must wear your rue with a difference. – There's a daisy: – I would give you some violets, but they withere'd all when my father died: – they say he made a good end."

(OPHELIA *wanders around the pool softly singing to herself, as* JESUS *prays with rising terror.*)

ROZ. Jesus, Hay-zoos, take it easy! It's not the Virgin Mary, it's Ophelia. You know, from "Hamlet"…"To be or not to be"…The Shakespeare play! She's a vision, an apparition…Like how the Virgin Mary shows up from time to time. But she's not *actually* the Virgin Mary, but a sort of stand in, a kind of…understudy. But Ophelia showing up is *truly* miraculous because she never existed! She's just a character in a play!

(JESUS *starts beating himself with a towel.*)

ROZ. You *do* know who Ophelia is, don't you? Hamlet's girlfriend who went mad and drowned herself after he accidentally killed her father…One minute he's swearing eternal love to her and the next he's raving like a maniac! *The poor thing never had a chance!* He used her!

(OPHELIA *finishes her song and stops dead. She gazes at them, totally disoriented.*)

ROZ. It's OK, honey, you're in the Galaxy Health Club in New York City. *Anno domini* 2009.* Calm down, nobody's going to hurt you. You're safe here. Just don't spend too much time in the whirlpool, it'll wreck havoc with your Elizabethan immune system.

OPHELIA. *(staring at JESUS' bathing suit)* My Lord Hamlet?

ROZ. Guess again. Your brother killed the bastard in a duel.

JESUS. I'm Hay-zoos...the life guard.

OPHELIA. Prithee, cover thyself, Sirrah.

JESUS. *(quickly covering his groin with his hands)* Hay-zoos Eduardo de Los Angeles Avila Morales.

ROZ. Could he and Laertes just sit down over a frosty glass of mead and settle their differences like civilized human beings? No, they had to fight! Because that's what men do! Fight and go whoring after innocent girls! Don't get me started... It was one thing when Wally went after his receptionist, but a checkout girl at Duane Reade! *(pause)* Who the hell *was* Duane Reade anyway?

OPHELIA. *(singing to JESUS, suddenly flirtatious)*
"By Gis and by Saint Charity,
Alack, and fie for shame!
Young men will do't, if they come to' it;
By cock, they are to blame.
Quoth she, before you tumbled me,
You promised me to wed."

JESUS. *(backing away from her)* Miss, Miss, you're mixing me up with someone else.

*(**OPHELIA**, who's subject to rapid mood changes, suddenly flies at JESUS and tries to scratch out his eyes.)*

OPHELIA. Thou dids't my noble father murder most foully! Fie on thee, Hamlet, fie! Good Polonius is dead!

JESUS. *(Trying to defend himself. In Spanish:)* Hey, watch it! You almost scratched out my eye! I didn't do anything. You're one crazy lady!

*****NOTE:** Performers should ammend this date to the year of their perfomance.

OPHELIA. Murderer most foul! I smell my father's blood on thy wicked hands. Release me, I say, release me!

(They struggle.)

JESUS. *(letting her go)* OK, OK...

ROZ. *(in a stage whisper to JESUS)* She's mad.

JESUS. What did I do?

ROZ. Not *angry* mad, *crazy* mad!

(ROZ rubs her finger on her lips making crazy person sounds. JESUS imitates her, unsure of her meaning.)

OPHELIA. *(rushing to the whirlpool to clean herself)* And now my flesh bears the marks o' your villainous hands.

ROZ. Nuts! Bonkers! *(circling her finger next to her ear in another crazy person gesture)* Forget it, forget it. Don't even try to reach her. You live in different worlds. *(putting her hand in the whirlpool)* Well what do you know? The heat came back. *(She turns on the jets and sinks down into the water.)* Ahhhhh, this is more like it. *(motioning to OPHELIA)* Come on in and join me.

(OPHELIA tentatively gets back into the pool. ROZ smiles at her and rests her arms on the edge. OPHELIA rests her arms on the edge. ROZ does head rolls. OPHELIA does head rolls. Then she starts singing again, tossing flowers into the water.)

OPHELIA. "He is dead and gone, lady
He is dead and gone;
At his head a grass-green turf,
At his heels a stone."

JESUS. *(rushing over to the whirlpool)* Miss, Miss, it's against the rules to throw flowers in the pool. You'll jam the filters.

(OPHELIA darts up to the rim of the pool and throws in more flowers.)

JESUS. *(grabbing her around the waist)* Miss, please!

(He places her back down on the floor. Feeling his arms around her, she guides him into a brief courtly dance.)

OPHELIA. *(suddenly pulling away)* Lord Hamlet, thou art much changed!

JESUS. My name is Hay-zoos...Hay-zoos Eduardo de Los Angeles Avila Morales. I'm the lifeguard here. I save the drowning. Whether they walk on land, swim the seas, or fly above. *(A pause, then he bows and does a poignant bird call.)*

OPHELIA. Thou know'st the song o' the meadow lark!

(JESUS sings like a tortoise.)

OPHELIA. The ancient tortoise!

(JESUS sings like a lizard.)

OPHELIA. The lowly lizard!

(JESUS sings like a porpoise.)

OPHELIA. *(clapping her hands with delight)* And e'en the paddle-billed porpoise.

(She joins him and they sing a poignant duet together)

JESUS. I know these songs because I was born in Costa Rica. My father was a fisherman. He caught more fish than anyone in our village. And do you know why? Because he couldn't speak like other men. He was born without a tongue. So he sharpened his ears and learned how to listen. He could hear the rain before it fell, the birds gossiping in distant jungles and the fish murmuring on the ocean floor. When he set sail in the morning, the gulls would lead him to his catch. The moment he dropped anchor, he dove into the water and swam with the very fish he was trying to lure into his nets. They told him their stories – about their ancestors who walked on land and their great cities that mysteriously sank into the sea. When I turned 12, he let me swim with him and taught me how to listen as well. Soon I was swimming great distances because the fish would guide me – showing me the safest routes and warning me of approaching storms. They'd sing to me when I got weary and spin tales about the ancient gods that once ruled the earth. Everyone thinks I swim for the glory of the miles I cover, but I do it because I long to be with the creatures of the deep. They entertain me, teach me and finally make me a better man.

OPHELIA. *(with sudden gravity)* Dost thou believe, my lord?

JESUS. Believe what?

OPHELIA. In a heart that's pure?

ROZ. *(under her breath)* Lotsa luck!

OPHELIA. I did possess one once, but then lost it.

JESUS. Where did you lose it?

OPHELIA. If I knew, t'would not be lost, my lord. And you?

JESUS. What about me?

OPHELIA. Where is thy heart?

JESUS. *(after a brief pause)* In your hands.

(**ROZ** *mimes playing a violin.*)

JESUS. All I've ever cared about was swimming, but now that I've met you…I…I…

OPHELIA. *(excited)* Thou swim'st?

JESUS. Great distances. Next month I attempt the English Channel.

OPHELIA. The *English*, Channel, my lord? In faith, I've crossed it oft!

JESUS. Thou swim'st too? I knew it! I knew it!

OPHELIA. *(momentarily lucid)* No, my lord, I crossed it in a ship. In my youth our family summered oft in England. We traveled by coach to Calais and thence set sail for Dover. Verily, they were the happiest o' times… Laertes and I wouldst clamber to the top o' the crow's nest and there peruse the changing horizon. At eventide, our father, good Polonius joined us in our swaying perch. He knew each constellation's place and wouldst point them out to us. *(as Polonius)* "There's Orion's Belt, mark it well…! And there, wretched Callisto, the great bear who weeps for her son, she unwittingly slayed with her own hand." Laertes and I hung on every word, his voice sinking and rising wi' the swells that bore us o'er the waves. Verily, he conversed wi' the wind itself, waving his arms as if swapping tales wi' a dear old friend. Twas he, my star-gazing father, who unfurled the twin maps that bind the earth – the constellations that wink above and the oceans that slumber below. Twas those very maps that guided me 'neath the waters o' the earth til I popped of a sudden into this...bubbling pool. *(She returns to the pool and gazes into its depths.)*

JESUS. Marry me!

OPHELIA. My lord?

JESUS. You're my other half! The bride I've been waiting for. *(He gently kisses her.)*

OPHELIA. *(moving away from him)* My lord!

JESUS. My father told me I'd find you one day.

OPHELIA. In faith, I didst love thee once.

JESUS. Together we'll swim the waters of the earth!

OPHELIA. But then thou came'st to me in my closet,
..."like sweet bells jangled, out of tune and harsh..."

JESUS. "Sweet bells jangled?"

OPHELIA. "That unmatcht form and feature of blown youth Blasted with ecstasy..."

JESUS. Yes, ecstasy! Ecstasy!

OPHELIA. *(pulling away)* "O woe is me, t'have seen what I have seen, see what I see."

JESUS. I don't care where I swim anymore – the Indian Ocean or the Dead Sea... I just want to be at your side. Hand in hand. Seeing together...listening together... moving through the water together...

(moving in to kiss her again)

ROZ. *(feigning a sudden asthma attack)* HELP...HELP... JESUS, I CAN'T BREATHE! I NEED MY INHALER! MY INHALER...

JESUS. *(rushing over to her)* Easy, easy, don't panic...

ROZ. *(gasping for air)* HURRY! MY INHALER...IT'S IN MY LOCKER...NUMBER 55... *(taking the keys off from around her wrist and throwing them at him)* HERE ARE THE KEYS. QUICKLY, QUICKLY...I CAN'T BREATHE...I can't breathe...

(She puts on quite a show, clutching her chest and making a variety of unearthly noises.)

JESUS. *(exiting as fast as he can)* Locker 55?

ROZ. Hurry... Hurry...

OPHELIA. *(bending over her)* My lady?

ROZ. *(recovering)* It's alright... I just wanted to get rid of him. "Too much of water hast thou poor Ophelia." You need a rest! Not some hot blooded marathon swimmer to drag you all over the map. And who's to say he wouldn't ditch you for some hot little mermaid sunning herself off a spit of sand on St. Tropez. You'd be better off on dry land... With Duane Reade! *(pause)* Him again! Why does his name keep coming up? Because his drug stores are on every goddamned street corner. Talk about overkill...! Men! Take my advice and forget the lot of them! *(grabbing her arm and speaking with great authority as Hamlet)* "Get thee to a nunnery."

OPHELIA. Why are those words so familiar? Verily, Hamlet spake them to me, 'nary a moment ago!

ROZ. I didn't get a chronic asthma condition teaching Shakespeare in the public school system for nothing! *(leading **OPHELIA** back into the whirlpool)* "Why wouldst thou be a breeder of sinners? I am myself indifferent honest: but yet I could accuse me of such things that it were better my mother had not borne me...I am very proud, revengful, ambitious; with more offences at my beck than I have thoughts to put them in, imagination to give them shape, or time to act them in. What should such fellows as I do crawling between earth and heaven? We are arrant knaves, all; believe none of us. Go thy ways to a nunnery...If thou dost marry, I'll give thee this plague for thy dowry, – be thou as chaste as ice, as pure as snow, thou shalt not escape calumny. Get thee to a nunnery, go: farewell..." *(as herself again, pushing* **OPHELIA** *under water)* I'm doing this for your own good, believe me!

OPHELIA. *(disappearing)* "I thank you for your good counsel. Come, my coach! – Good night ladies; good night sweet ladies: good night, good night." *(And she's gone.)*

ROZ. Now...how do you drain this damned thing? There must be a plug somewhere on the bottom...Ah here it is! *(She dramatically pulls it out.)*

(There's a terrific sound of water slurping down the drain. **ROZ** *struggles not to be sucked down as well.)*

JESUS. *(from offstage)* I'VE GOT IT! I'VE GOT YOUR INHALER! YOU MUST HAVE GIVEN ME YOUR HOUSE KEYS BY MISTAKE.

*(***ROZ*** quickly sneaks out of the room.)*

JESUS. I COULDN'T OPEN THE LOCK AND HAD TO BREAK DOWN THE DOOR! *(running in)* Hey, where did everybody go? *(rushing into the whirlpool)* Ophelia... Ophelia... Where are you? What happened to all the water? *(breaking down, speaking in Spanish as the swooning Allegro molto from Handel's Suite #1 starts to play:)* Ophelia, Ophelia, come back! I love you! We were going to swim the oceans together... You're my other half... my shining starfish, my plunging porpoise, my watery bride...I feel through your hands, sing through your voice and breathe through your lungs. Ophelia, Ophelia, save me...I'm drowning...*

(The lights slowly fade on his heartbroken face.)

End of Play

* *(Spanish translation:)* Ofelia, Ofelia, regressa! Te amo. Ibamos a nadar las aguas del mundo, mi media naranja, mi novia acuatica, mi delfin del fondo, mi estrellita del mar. Con tus manos siento, con tu boca canto, y con tus pulmones respiro. Ofelia, Ofelia, Salvame! Que me ahogo!

THROUGH A GLASS DARKLY

CHARACTERS

DR. NIKOLAI CHEKHOV – An ophthalmologist, 40s
KITTY BRIGHT – his patient, a playwright, 30s

SETTING

Dr. Chekhov's examining room which can be evoked by an eye chart and a few lurid close-ups of the structure of the eye. There's a chair for him and large reclining chair for the patient.

(AT RISE: **DR. CHEKHOV** *is standing at the door calling for his next patient.)*

DR. CHEKHOV. Miss Bright? *(pause)* Miss Bright? *(longer pause, then stepping out of the office)* Miss Bright? Where are you?

KITTY. *(offstage, shaking the door)* In the restroom! I'm locked in!

DR. CHEKHOV. Excuse me?

KITTY. I said, I'm locked in the restroom! *(shaking the door harder)* I can't find the lock because of the damned drops you put in!

DR. CHEKHOV. *(overlapping)* You've got to stop that banging! I can't hear a word you're saying!

KITTY. *(shaking the door)* I SAID I CAN'T SEE THE LOCK…! THE LOCK! THE LOCK! EVERYTHING'S A BLUR!

DR. CHEKHOV. *(exiting)* Calm down, Miss Bright, I'm right here, I'll talk you through it.

(She mews, kicking the door throughout.)

Just slide your hands down the door and see if you can feel the lock. Miss Bright? Miss Bright? *(pause)* Can you feel it? *(silence)* Miss Bright, are you still alive?

KITTY. I found it!

DR. CHEKHOV. Good girl. Now push it like you'd push a button in an elevator and the door should open.

(More mewing, she bursts out, spinning like a top.)

DR. CHEKHOV. Finally! For a minute there, I thought we'd have to call the fire department! This way…Over here, Miss Bright.

(He re-enters the room, backwards. **KITTY** *follows, trailing a long train of toilet paper from her shoe.)*

KITTY. *(skidding to a stop, covering her eyes with her hands.)*

WOA! IT'S SO BRIGHT! I forgot how these drops do that to you! *(creeping in, feeling the walls)*

DR. CHEKHOV. *(leading her towards the examining chair)* Easy, easy...this way... Just follow me.

KITTY. *(plopping into the chair)* And of course I forgot to bring sunglasses for when I leave. Unless...unless...I have a pair in here... God knows, I have everything else! *(opening her bulging hand bag and plowing through it)*

DR. CHEKHOV. Don't worry, I'll lend you a pair.

*(**KITTY** hauls out a bathing cap, goggles, nose clip, small hair dryer, styling mousse and pair of binoculars which invariably tumble to the floor as she scrambles to retrieve them.)*

KITTY. This has not been my day. First my vision goes haywire, then I forget to bring sunglasses for the goddamned drops.

*(Overlapping as **DR. CHEKHOV** tries to pull the tail of toilet paper off her shoe.)*

DR. CHEKHOV. Excuse me, but I think you...*(bumping into her)* Whoops, sorry, sorry...I think you might have... um...stepped on something...

KITTY. *(squinting over at him)* What is that? I can't see a thing!

DR. CHEKHOV. *(Quickly gathering it up and scrunching it into a ball, he aims for the wastepaper basket and misses.)* Rats!

KITTY. *(shooting up from the chair, alarmed)* Rats?

DR. CHEKHOV. *(picking it up and placing it in the basket)* That's what I get for skipping the gym this week...Serves me right.

KITTY. You saw *rats?*

DR. CHEKHOV. *(easing her back into the chair)* No, Miss Bright, no rats. We keep *very* clean offices here. So...let's find out what seems to be the problem...

(He pushes a button that makes her chair recline backwards.)

KITTY. *(her hands shooting up in the air)* Woa!

DR. CHEKHOV. You said something about holes in your vision…

KITTY. I think it's a torn retina. My mother had one once. As she was shopping at Gristedes, this enormous octopus suddenly floated across the produce aisle…The doctor said her retina had become detached. I don't see an octopus, it's more like things…disintegrating.

DR. CHEKHOV. OK, Miss Bright, I'm going to put some more drops in your eyes.

KITTY. More drops?

DR. CHEKHOV. Just to numb them. It'll sting for a second, then you won't feel a thing. *(He puts them in.)*

*(*KITTY *gasps.)*

DR. CHEKHOV. You were saying?

KITTY. I was trying to describe what's been going on. It's hard because it's so…*weird!*

DR. CHEKHOV. Well, if anyone can describe it, you can! I'm a huge fan of your work.

KITTY. You know my plays?

DR. CHEKHOV. My wife and I have seen every one.

KITTY. Dr. Chekhov, I don't know what to say!

DR. CHEKHOV. "Red x 3," "Darwin's Ear," "Between the Bed and the Table"…That scene where the little girl pulled the dove out of her shirt…

KITTY. Yeah, that was…

DR. CHEKHOV. And then started to fly around the room after it…How did you do that?

KITTY. Smoke and mirrors, smoke and mirrors…

DR. CHEKHOV. I still dream about it.

KITTY. Yeah, theater can be pretty amazing. Speaking of which…your name…everyone must ask you… Are you related to *the* Anton Chekhov?

DR. CHEKHOV. *(world weary)* Here we go…

KITTY. Well, if *my* last name were Shakespeare, wouldn't you want to know if we were related? *(pause)* So…*Are* you?

DR. CHEKHOV. *(softly)* As a matter of fact, I am.

KITTY. *(sitting up and grabbing his hand)* Oh, Dr. Chekhov, I'm so honored to meet you.

DR. CHEKHOV. Distantly. Very distantly.

KITTY. I adore Chekhov's plays. He's the best, the best!

DR. CHEKHOV. Why thank you.

KITTY. Do you write too?

(He laughs wistfully.)

KITTY. Well *do* you?

DR. CHEKHOV. I try...

(long pause)

KITTY. *(getting more excited)* Short stories or plays?

*(***DR. CHEKHOV** *sighs wistfully.)*

KITTY. Tell me, tell me!

DR. CHEKHOV. *(smiling sheepishly, dropping his eyes)* I belong to a writer's group at the hospital.

KITTY. Doctors meet to write *plays*?

DR. CHEKHOV. We're not very good.

KITTY. But that's so touching!

DR. CHEKHOV. *(increasingly upset)* In fact, we're all terrible. *(a pause)* Enough, enough. I don't want to talk about it.

KITTY. I'm sorry, I didn't mean to intrude.

(long pause)

DR. CHEKHOV. *(all business again)* So, where were we?

KITTY. You wanted me to describe what's been going on.

DR. CHEKHOV. Right, right...But before you tell me, I'm going to pop this stick of dentine gum in my mouth to mask the tuna fish sandwich I had for lunch, *(he does)* and then I'm going to insert this little magnifying device into your eye...But first, I have to flip your eyelid back. *(He does.)*

KITTY. Ah!

DR. CHEKHOV. *(His face in hers as he examines her.)* Please continue, Miss Bright..

KITTY. Woa...! *(taking a deep breath)* OK...imagine that everything you see is a jig saw puzzle made of millions of teeny tiny pieces and then the pieces in the middle start to crumble and disappear...

DR. CHEKHOV. *(getting closer and closer to her)* Mmm... mmmm...

KITTY. I was at rehearsal of my new play yesterday when the face of the lead actress started to fall apart... It just... disintegrated in front of my eyes... Like right now, there's a hole where you should be.

DR. CHEKHOV. *(continuing to examine her)* Mmm... mmm...

(time passes)

KITTY. So, what's wrong? Do you see anything? Is my retina detached?

DR. CHEKHOV. So far, so good...Now I'm going to shine a light in your eye for a better look. It will be quite bright, but try and stay with me. *(turning it on)* Look up, please.

KITTY. *(pulling away)* Ahhh, it's blinding!

DR. CHEKHOV. I know, I know...Let me help by explaining a bit about the physics of seeing...Light rays enter the eye and converge on the retina, where an upside-down image is created...Very good! Now look down...

KITTY. Oooh...ahhh...aieeee...ohhhh... *(overlapping)*

DR. CHEKHOV. The retina of each eye relays impulses to the brain through the optic nerves, which cross paths at a junction called the...

KITTY. Oooh...eeee...la la la la la...ma ma ma ma... *(overlapping)*

DR. CHEKHOV. *(soldiering on) Optic chiasm!* And now to the right...Well done, Miss Bright. You're doing beautifully, beautifully! Half the nerve fibers from the right eye cross to the left and vice versa, before passing on to the brain. Now look to the left.

(She starts mewing as)

DR. CHEKHOV. The image is then turned upright in the

visual cortex. Very good! And now the other eye.

KITTY. *(weakly)* The other eye?

DR. CHEKHOV. *(taking the magnifying device out of her right eye, flipping her lid on the left eye and placing it in)* Well, you do have two of them, don't you? Alright, Miss Bright, look up please.

(Her mewing, panting and gurgling reaches new levels.)

DR. CHEKHOV. *(appearing to be eating her alive)* There are two types of nerve cells in the retina: rods and cones... and now down...Rods contain only one type of light-sensitive pigment, and cannot discern color...To the right please...Cones, on which color vision depends, are of three classes that respond to green, red, or blue light...and now to the left...

*(***KITTY** *passes out.)*

DR. CHEKHOV. I said to the left...Miss Bright...yoo hoooooo? Did you hear me? Hellllooooo...Miss Bright? *(no response)* Oh no, she must have passed out! *(listening to her heart)* Well at least she's still alive, that's a relief! *(gently slapping her face)* Miss Bright, Miss Bright...wake up.

*(***KITTY** *slides deeper into the chair.)*

DR. CHEKHOV. Well, this is a first. What do I do now? Miss Bright? Miss Bright? Think, Nikoli, *think!* Be creative for once in your life! How does one wake a sleeping damsel? *(pause)* Why, with a kiss of course...But then I'd get slapped with a malpractice suit. She and her lawyers would take me to the cleaners! *(shaking her harder)* Miss Bright? *(in a sing song)* Oh Miss Briiii-iight? Wake uuuuu-uuuup! *(staring at her, at a loss)* Oh what the hell, she's in the theater and my name is Chekhov.

(He leans over her and gives her a sweet kiss on the lips. She wakes.)

KITTY. *(Groggy)* Where am I?

DR. CHEKHOV. *(leaping away from her)* Miss Bright, thank God!

KITTY. What happened?

DR. CHEKHOV. I'm afraid you passed out.

KITTY. I just had the strangest dream…I dreamed I was sleeping in a glass coffin in the middle of a meadow… when a knight in armor came galloping by. He dismounted, opened the lid of my coffin, raised his visor and gave me this lovely kiss that tasted like cinnamon… *(licking her lips)* Ohhh…mmmmm… It was the most delicious kiss I ever tasted…

DR. CHEKHOV. *(wiping his mouth)* A kiss?… In my office… Well, well, what do you know…?

(a slight pause)

KITTY. So, what did you find?

DR. CHEKHOV. *(lost)* Find?

KITTY. About my eyes.

DR. CHEKHOV. *(coming to)* Your eyes, your eyes! Right! Both retinas are fine.

KITTY. They're not torn or detached?

DR. CHEKHOV. They're as healthy as the day is long.

KITTY. Ohh, what a relief!

DR. CHEKHOV. Congratulations.

KITTY. Wait a minute! So why was there a hole in everything I saw. *(pause)* Oh God… I don't have a brain tumor, do I?

DR. CHEKHOV. No, no. It was a migraine aura.

KITTY. A migraine aura, what's that?

DR. CHEKHOV. A visual disturbance that occurs when there's drop in the blood flow to your brain.

KITTY. So, what do I do if it happens again?

DR. CHEKHOV. Just take some Excedrin Migraine when you feel it coming on. If it gets worse, you see a neurologist.

KITTY. *(panicking)* A *neurologist?*

DR. CHEKHOV. *(taking her hand)* There, there, it's nothing to worry about, my wife gets them all the time.

KITTY. Really?

DR. CHEKHOV. At least twice a week.

KITTY. Could I just ask you one last rather...strange question?

DR. CHEKHOV. Anything, Miss Bright... Anything.

KITTY. When you were peering into my eyes with that light...could you...could you... Now please don't laugh... But...could you...see into my soul?

DR. CHEKHOV. See into your *soul?*

KITTY. The light was so bright and went so deep, I was sure you could.

DR. CHEKHOV. *(with rising excitement)* See into your soul?

KITTY. Come on, fess up. You saw it all. The whole heaving mess.

DR. CHEKHOV. *(whispering)* The laughing exit signs...

KITTY. The murmuring umbrellas...

KITTY & DR. CHEKHOV. The flying babies...

DR. CHEKHOV. Oh, Miss Bright, I've been waiting for that question all my life! Of course I can see into your soul, just as I can see into the souls of *all* my patients – the lost children, the blood on the faucets, the weeping silverware...

KITTY. The headless women...

DR. CHEKHOV. All that snow...

KITTY. Can't see for miles...

DR. CHEKHOV. The roads are closed...

KITTY. Dead silence...

(a pause)

DR. CHEKHOV. And then the visions start...

KITTY. *(taking his hand)* I want to read your plays, Dr. Chekhov...

DR. CHEKHOV. The lawns and feathered hats... The kisses and farewells...

KITTY. I want to read them all!

DR. CHEKHOV. *(moving away from her, waving, as a character* *in his play)* "Goodbye…goodbye…goodbye, my love. Until we meet again… Farewell."

(He stops, then turns to look at her. Hand over her heart, she smiles at him, eyes brimming.)

End of Play

SKIN DEEP

CHARACTERS

DR. MARVELL – A dermatologist, 40s, 50s
DAPHNE – A beautiful nymph on the run, 20s
APOLLO – A Greek god, 20s, 30s
VOICE OF THE CONDUCTOR

SETTING

The interior of an R train in New York City. It should have a vaguely dream-like, unfinished feel.

(*AT RISE:* **DR. MARVELL**, *a nondescript man sits under the only ad in the train, his own, promising "Your skin will glow, your age won't show" along with other verses. He's dressed exactly as he appears in his ad, wearing a white doctor's jacket with a stethoscope poking out of his pocket. The train stops.*)

VOICE OF CONDUCTOR. 8th Street. This is a Brooklyn Bound Local R train. Next stop, Prince Street. Stand clear of the closing door please.

(**DR. MARVELL** *looks up waiting to be recognized, but no one enters. He stays put, hoping for better luck at the next stop. The doors finally open at the next stop.*)

VOICE OF CONDUCTOR. Station stop Prince Street. Next stop Canal. Stand clear of the closing doors please.

(*No one enters. Just as the doors are about to close,* **DAPHNE** *rushes in barefoot, terrified and out of breath. She's in her 20s and very beautiful, with long blonde hair that swirls around her. She wears a classic Greek tunic and has a vaguely greenish cast to her skin. Someone's clearly hot on her heels*)

APOLLO'S VOICE. (*getting weaker as the train speeds away*) I walk in a tower of flames…I burn for you…I am consumed…Come back, come back, come back, come baaaaaaaaack…

DAPHNE. (*throwing herself at* **DR. MARVELL**) Helllllp! Helllp! Save me!

DR. MARVELL. Hey, hey, take it easy…

DAPHNE. SAVE ME!

DR. MARVELL. You lost him.

DAPHNE. That's what you think.

DR. MARVELL. He's toast.

DAPHNE. I'm a goner. He's very fast.

DR. MARVELL. No one's fast enough to outrun the R train. Except for Superman.

DAPHNE. *(gasping for breath)* Superman?

DR. MARVELL. *(gesturing towards a seat across from him)* You'd better sit down.

(DAPHNE crawls to the other end of the car, trying not to be seen through the window or doors.)

DR. MARVELL. What are you doing? And your shoes! What happened to your shoes?

(She finally sits down with her head in her hands.)

I know it's none of my business, but you shouldn't be running around the subway, barefoot. God knows what you might step in! Or on! Carpet tacks…Thumbtacks…Backpacks…Knick-knacks *(getting lost in a verbal tic)*…Cracker Jacks…six packs…Hunchbacks…Lumberjacks…Maniacs…

(DAPHNE starts to sob.)

DR. MARVELL. *(walking over to her, gently touching her shoulder)* Hey, hey…

DAPHNE. *(whirling away from him)* TAKE. YOUR. HANDS. OFF. OF. ME!

DR. MARVELL. *(backing off)* Easy, easy, I was just trying to…

DAPHNE. Father, Father! I want my father!

DR. MARVELL. Calm down…

DAPHNE. PENEUS, GREAT RIVER GOD THAT CUTS A WATERY PATH PAST MOUNT OLYMPUS DOWN TO THE AEGEAN SEA. STILL YOUR CLAMBERING CURRENTS AND HEAR ME!

DR. MARVELL. Alright, Miss…let's just…Calm. Down. Take a deep breath… *(He does.)*

(She does.)

DR. MARVELL. Atta girl, now slowly let it out…

(She does.)

DR. MARVELL. Good girl! And again.

(They continue breathing deeply together.)

DR. MARVELL. I'm a doctor.

DAPHNE. A doctor?

(**DR. MARVELL** *returns to his seat and sits squarely under his ad. He points up to it and smiles.*)

DAPHNE. *(looking at the ad, then at him, then at the ad again)* No! That's you!

DR. MARVELL. *(with a little bow)* Dr. Joel Marvell, Board certified dermatologist, at your service. I treat the skin.

DAPHNE. The epidermis!

DR. MARVELL. *(pulling on his cheek)* Yes, the epidermis that sheathes your entire body. The largest of all our organs.

DAPHNE. *(innocently running her hands down her body)* That sheathes my entire body…

DR. MARVELL. I remove blemishes and freckles, restoring skin to its youthful luster.

DAPHNE. *(reading his sign)* "Blemishes and moles a thing of the past, radiant skin will be yours at last."

DR. MARVELL. My office is centrally located and I take all forms of insurance.

DAPHNE. *(reading)* "Free consultations, competitive rates, walk-ins accepted, and no long waits."

DR. MARVELL. I wrote that copy myself. When I was in medical school I had dreams of being a poet as well. You know, like William Carlos Williams. *(reciting)* "By the road to the contagious hospital under the surge of the blue mottled clouds driven from the northeast – a cold wind."

(*The lights suddenly go out.*)

DR. MARVELL. *(world weary)* There go the damn lights again! Let's hear it for the good old M.T.A.

DAPHNE. M.T.A.?

DR. MARVELL. The Metropolitan Transit Authority. *(like a cheerleader)* Give me an "M."

DAPHNE. "M"?

DR. MARVELL. Give me a "T."

DAPHNE. "T"?

DR. MARVELL. Give me an "A."

DAPHNE. "A"?

DR. MARVELL. And what have you got?

DAPHNE. I don't know.

DR. MARVELL. M.T.A!

DAPHNE. M.T.A?

DR. MARVELL. *(with brio)* M.T.A. U.J.A. A.M.A.

DAPHNE. *(trying to imitate his spirit)* T.G.A. Q.P.A Z.D.A.

DR. MARVELL. A.S.P.C.A.

DAPHNE. D.L.R.X.A.!

APOLLO'S VOICE. *(in the distance)* Daphneeee... Daphneeeeeee!

DAPHNE. He's back. What did I tell you?

APOLLO'S VOICE. Your beauty burns like a thousand suns. I am scorched. Ashes fall from my mouth.

*(The lights come back on. **DAPHNE**'s skin is greener than before.)*

DAPHNE. *(groaning, slumping down in her seat)* Uuuugh, I don't feel well.

DR. MARVELL. You don't look so good either. Could you describe your symptoms for me?

DAPHNE. I feel heavy, weighted down...As if my arms and legs were made of wood!

DR. MARVELL. The moment you entered the car, I noticed a greenish cast to your skin – the kind of Verdant Dermatitis that accompanies motion sickness, but it seems to be getting worse.

DAPHNE. *(slurring her words)* I'm so sleepy all of a sudden, I can hardly move.

DR. MARVELL. *(approaching her)* Fortunately, I always carry my bag with me. May I?

(He takes her pulse, listens to her heart and lungs with his stethoscope, depresses her tongue and taps her knee with one of those weird little hammers.)

DR. MARVELL. Just as I suspected. This is not good, not good at all! You need to get to a hospital right away.

DAPHNE. *(slumping down over several seats)* A hospital?

DR. MARVELL. *(running his hand over her legs)* Your skin feels so rough – like sand paper or corrugated cardboard – as if you're in the early stages of Elephantiasis, or Staten Island Lyme Disease.

DAPHNE. *(weaker still)* Staten Island Lyme Disease?

DR. MARVELL. *(whipping a digital camera out of his bag and snapping pictures of her)* Do you mind? *(taking her blood pressure)* Your vital signs are going haywire! Blood pressure 13 over 150…No, make that 80 over 4…No, 24/7 over 365.

DAPHNE. *(overlapping him)* FATHER! IF YOU LOVE ME, RISE UP FROM YOUR TUMBLING STREAMS AND SAVE ME!

DR. MARVELL. *(pulling out a little notebook or tape recorder)* Alright, Daphne, I need to ask you a few questions here.

DAPHNE. *(suddenly lifting her head)* Do you smell…bay leaves?

(a pause as he sniffs)

DR. MARVELL. Do you have any allergies or family history of high blood pressure, circulatory problems, heart disease or mental illness?

DAPHNE. I was running in the park, hunting the animals.

DR. MARVELL. Hunting the animals…

DAPHNE. Mostly rabbits and deer.

DR. MARVELL. Rabbits and deer…

DAPHNE. I love animals!

DR. MARVELL. Me too! Mrs. Marvell and I have cats. Mimi… Echo… Mr. Pettibone…

DAPHNE. Their coats are so sleek and fragrant. Like flowers kissed by morning dew. Each species has its own aroma… Does – honeyed freesia… Lambs – tender violets, and rabbits, rabbits – they make me so dizzy, words fail!

(slight pause)

DR. MARVELL. So...you were in the park...hunting rabbits and deer...when this fellow started chasing you. Is this guy your boyfriend?

(The lights go out again. **DAPHNE** *screams.)*

DR. MARVELL. There they go again! Unbelievable!

DAPHNE. Ughh! I hate men!

DR. MARVELL. Interesting, interesting... Go on.

DAPHNE. As I was running after a doe, I saw this boy...man, really...sitting under a tree playing a lyre and the next thing I knew he was chasing me, his hot breath singeing my neck and shoulders... *(shuddering)* He smelled like a rotting centaur carcass.

VOICE OF CONDUCTOR. Station is Canal Street, transfer available for the N and Q, the downtown 6,J,M,Z. Next stop City Hall. Stand clear of the closing doors please.

APOLLO'S VOICE. Oh daughter of the deep green-shadowed River,

Who follows you is not your enemy...

(The lights come back on. Twigs and leaves are sprouting out of her tunic.)

DR. MARVELL. Sweet Christ, what's happening to you? *(snapping more pictures of her)*

DAPHNE. *(barely audible)* Ohhhh, I feel so heavy I can hardly speak.

(The train stops.)

VOICE OF CONDUCTOR. City Hall Station. This train bypassing Courtland Street. Next stop, Rector. Stand clear of the closing doors please.

(The door opens and **APOLLO** *enters in a blaze of light and heavenly music. He's wildly handsome, dressed in a tunic and carrying a lyre. He rushes to* **DAPHNE.** *A lopsided chase ensues due to her encroaching stiffness. He finally catches her and lifts her aloft in the pose of Bernini's "***APOLLO** *and* **DAPHNE.***")*

APOLLO. *(putting her down and covering her with kisses)*
The lamb runs from the wolf, the deer from the lion,

The trembling-feathered dove flies from the eagle
Whose great wings cross the sky – such is your flight
While mine is love's pursuit!

(He struggles to lift her up again, but she's rooted to the floor, arms aloft.)

DR. MARVELL. Hands off! Who do you think you are? This woman is sick. She needs medical attention and she needs it NOW!

(The lights start to flicker.)

DAPHNE. Father, if your waters still hold charms
To save your daughter, cover with green earth
This body I wear too well.

(There's an intergalactic sound and lighting effect only a river god could make.)

DR. MARVELL. *(to APOLLO)* You may think you're some super hero, strutting around in a fancy costume with your own private lighting effect, but I happen to be a level nine red belt in Karate! You're dealing with a master Karateka here! They don't call me Dr. Marvell for nothing! *(whipping off his jacket revealing his karate belt, striking a pose and emitting a fearful yell)*
(The lights go out completely and the two fight in darkness. We hear terrible grunts and blows, accompanied by a subway drummer.)

DR. MARVELL.	**APOLLO.**
(more karate yells) Jesus Christ, what's happened to security in this city? When you get on a train you take your life in your hands! What was I thinking? What am I doing here?	Unhand me, you fool! Jove is my father and I am the lord of Delphi. My temples stand at Claros, Patara and beyond the cities, glimmering Tenebros, enchanted islands of the eastern seas.

(Normal lighting returns. The two lie crumpled on the floor. **APOLLO** *is out cold and* **DAPHNE** *has been replaced by a laurel tree.)*

DAPHNE'S VOICE. *(from far away)* Give me an M. Give me a T. Give me an A...What have you got?

DR. MARVELL. *(looking around the car)* Where did she go? Wait a minute...Wait just...One. Cotton. Picking. Minute... spinnet, linnet, plinnet, zinnet! There's a tree growing in the middle of the car and I'll bet you dollars to donuts it's a laurel! *(examining it)* Just as I thought! Ovid's Daphne! So, you must be Apollo, the sun god... hot rod...pea pod...rough shod...Cape Cod! *(slapping his face)* Enough with the rhyming doggerel, Marvell, pull yourself together! This calls for the grandeur of blank verse... *(plucking off a handful of leaves and weaving them into a wreath)* And so your father heard you – rose from his watery bed, planted your feet in the ground, wrapped you in bark and crowned your head with laurel. Look at you...Just look at you! Ever green and ever young! No face lifts, eye tucks or boxtox for you, but deciduous perfection 'til the end of time. Athletes will circle their heads with your laurel and perfumers and chefs will extract your exotic oils... *(burying his head in her leaves)* Ahhh, the fragrances you toss from bough to bough – cinnamon, sassafras, and Old Spice...My head spins! *(placing the wreath on his head)* And so I'll follow you to the great park where you'll be planted near the animals you love...and Mimi, Echo and Mr. Pettibone will join me...We'll tend and comfort you as I stop passersby to recount your wondrous tale...

(He picks up his bag and heads out the door, his wreath bathed in light.)

(fainter and fainter) Of how a nymph leapt into the R train running from a god, and how she met a dermatologist on his way home after a long day of seeing patients...and how he noticed a greenish cast to her skin and proceeded to question her about her condition...and how she told him about her father, a river god, who cut a watery path past Mount Olympus down to the Aegean Sea...

End of Play

MILK & WATER

CHARACTERS

RO, the actress – wears a state of the art tank suit and matching cap.

CANADA, the doctor – wears a nice suit that's too big for her.

JOAN, the trader – wears makeup and a shockingly bright suit, probably with stripes.

APRIL, the poet – wears glasses, a shower cap and a totally woebegone suit, perhaps with its own skirt.

MAGDA, the Eastern European or Russian girl – wears a weird Eastern European suit and cap

WHAT'S HER NAME, who works at the front desk – wears sweats and sneakers

>All of the women should be of child-bearing age.

SETTING

A health club pool ringed with bins of weights, flippers and noodles. The pool itself is suggested by two red and white plastic lane dividers that run the length of the stage. To create the illusion of being buoyant, the actors should walk with gliding steps and move their upper bodies as if they're underwater. One could also stretch waist-high fluttering blue silk panels between the dividers to hide their legs. The lighting should have that weird indoor pool watery cast and be accompanied by a splashing, echoey soundscape.

(AT RISE: 6:50 a.m., an overcast day in March. **RO**, **JOAN**, **APRIL** *and* **CANADA** *have been in the pool for 20 minutes. They're up in arms because their water aerobics teacher is 20 minutes late.* **MAGDA**, *the Eastern European or Russian girl who barely speaks English, hovers nearby.)*

(speaking simultaneously:)

RO. *(looking at her watch)* Now she's twenty minutes late! TWENTY FRIGGIN' MINUTES! There goes my day!

JOAN. I don't know about the rest of you, but this is unacceptable, totally unacceptable! Where I work, time is money!

CANADA. Twenty minutes…half an hour…what difference does it make? My life is already impossible!

APRIL. No fair! If I'd known she was going to be late I could still be home, nursing!

MAGDA. *(All her lines should be translated into an Eastern European language or Russian.)* What happened to our teacher? Did the authorities take her away?

*(***WHAT'S HER NAME** *enters in street clothes.)*

RO. Uh oh, here comes what's her name from the front desk. What *is* her name?

JOAN. Don't ask me.

CANADA. Ila? Ilse? Elise?

*(***WHAT'S HER NAME** *blows a whistle.)*

RO.	**JOAN.**	**APRIL.**	**CANADA.**
Brace yourself!	Finally!	Here we go!	Easy on the whistle!

WHAT'S HER NAME. I'm sorry ladies, but the Nursing Mothers' Water Aerobics Class is cancelled. I just got a call from Saviana. Her car broke down on the Jersey pike and she's stuck in Parsnippity.

RO.	JOAN.	APRIL.	CANADA.
Likely story!	Great! This is just great!	Is she alright?	Well, there goes my lunch hour!

RO. And I really needed a workout this morning!

CANADA. *You* needed a workout?

JOAN. What about me? The baby was up half the night!

RO. Mine never went to sleep!

APRIL. I woke mine up, I missed him so much.

RO, CANADA & JOAN. You're crazy!

APRIL. I love nursing!

CANADA. As did I, but my maternity leave is over, so it's back to delivering *other* women's babies – who keep streaming into the hospital in epic numbers!

JOAN. This is *not* turning out to be a good day!

RO. Try, *year*!

CANADA. I can't keep up!

JOAN. *You* can't keep up??? Two weeks ago I told my people to go short on Apple, anticipating weak earnings. After the market closed last night, they reported a 50% increase instead. Do you know how much money my clients are going to lose?

RO. I can't even remember the last time I worked!

JOAN. We're talking *millions!*

CANADA. I already have six C sections lined up, and my covering doctor is out, so guess who'll be on call all night?

JOAN. I'm dead in the water!

RO. Tomorrow the baby and I are picking up stakes and heading out to L.A. for pilot season. This is it for my acting career! The last roll of the dice! *(She makes a dramatic sound effect.)*

APRIL. I haven't written a new poem in months, I'm so baby drunk! And you know what? I've never been happier!

WHAT'S HER NAME. *(exiting)* Sorry ladies. Have a nice day!

APRIL. *(clutching her breasts as milk drips into the water)* I've become this gigantic breast, spurting milk like some confused water hydrant. Look! *(swirling it around)*

(The others gather to look.)

RO.	**JOAN.**	**MAGDA.**	**CANADA.**
Woa…!	Far out!	Holy Christ!	That was me a month ago!

APRIL. Whenever I think about my precious little doodle bunny, out it pours! *(pulling a photo out of her bathing cap)* Look at my sweetie, just look at him!

(More milk gushes into the pool.)

RO.	**JOAN.**	**CANADA.**	**MAGDA.**
Awwww!	He's so cute!	Precious!	Look! Look!

*(**MAGDA** then pulls a plastic wrapped photo out of her suit.)*

RO.	**JOAN.**	**CANADA.**	**APRIL.**
Look at that smile!	Stop it!	Heaven, heaven!	Catch me before I faint…!

MAGDA. *(holding up six fingers)* Her name is Kasia, she is 6 months old!

(The others press their hearts and coo.)

APRIL. *(loud, flapping her arms as if **MAGDA** were deaf)* SHE'S AN ANGEL! JUST AN ANGEL!

MAGDA. *(putting the picture back in her suit, speaking pigeon English)* She was born in… *(naming an Eastern European or Russian city)* Rudi and I move here four months ago…He's civil engineer.

RO. So, what do we do now? We have the lane for another

half hour.

JOAN. How about laps?

RO. *Laps?* I need a real workout.

APRIL. *(thinking)* A workout, a workout…Wait just one broccoli picking minute…*You* be the teacher!

RO. Me?

APRIL. Yes, *you!* You're the star, after all.

RO. Some star…I can't get arrested!

CANADA.	**APRIL.**	**JOAN.**
Athlete…	Actress…	Goddess…

APRIL. Ro! Ro! We want Ro!

ALL. Ro! Ro! We want Ro! Ro! Ro! We want Ro! *(etc.)*

RO. OK, OK, you talked me into it. *(putting on an official voice)* Alright ladies, line up…How about we start with cross country ski?

ALL. *(cheering as they line up)* Cross country ski! Cross country ski! *(etc.)*

(With **RO** *in the lead they do cross country ski for a lap as…*)

RO. Extend those arms and legs and work that core! Extend…extend…

ALL. *(chanting)* Extend…extend…extend…extend… *(etc.)*

RO. Breast stroke with your arms…Now punch out…down to your side…and behind your back…Good! Touch your calves…your heels…Paddle wheel…Paddle wheel in the opposite direction…Nice. Very nice…

(*They do each of these moves for one lap, turning around at the end of the lane for the next one.*)

RO. *(mid lane)* Now turn around and go in the other direction moving against the current…And take that into jumping jacks, working your core…And now rocking horse, leading with your right foot…and now your left… Let's pick up speed…right, left, right, left, right, left…

ALL. *(going faster, falling out of sync)* Right, left, right, left, right, left… *(etc.)*

RO. Faster, faster…Lift those knees and work those abs!

JOAN.	**CANADA.**	**APRIL.**
Slow down, slow down!	Take it easy! Not so fast!	I'm going to have a heart attack!

RO. *(dragging the bin of styrofoam weights closer)* Alright ladies, time for weights so we can lift our own bags up into those naaasty overhead bins on airplanes! *(holding up a series of dark blue, light blue, yellow and mixed blue and yellow Styrofoam hand weights)* Who wants what color?

(waving their hands)

CANADA.	**JOAN.**	**APRIL.**
Dark blue, please.	Yellow, yellow!	Tutti-fruitti

*(**MAGDA** points to the light blue and **RO** hands them all out, taking a dark blue pair for herself.)*

RO. Now find yourself a spot and let's jog in place.

(They do.)

RO. Good. Now circle your arms…and the other way… Take that into a figure eight and now in the other direction…Good! Let's bring in the plane…*(She waves her arms in a variety of configurations and then starts chanting.)* Y.M.C.A.…

(They do these exercises in place, finally chanting and doing the Y.M.C.A. moves along with her.)

RO. Now onto the crab walk to work those quads and abs!

ALL. Crab walk, crab walk! We love the crab walk!

(They start gliding down the lane sideways in 5th position.)

RO. Place your right hand on your hip and raise your left hand eight times. Now place your left hand on your hip and raise your right hand eight times. Good! Now four times on each side…

(They chant "right" or "left" depending on where they are.)

RO. Now twice...now once, switching back and forth, left, right, left, right *(etc.)* Faster, Faster...Now punch both hands into the air and go as fast as you can. Come on, let's see some real speed here. Pretend you're running for a bus or the train...Or a *taxi!* With your baby under your arm...He's spiking a fever, so you're trying to get to the nearest emergency room. It's pouring rain – a howling thunder storm with blinding flashes of lighting, the whole ten yards. You're terrified he'll be struck in his tender little fontanel...You hail a cab... when some hot little starlet you recognize from TV, tries to beat you to it, yelling that she's late for her shoot, holding up the entire film crew...She's gaining on you! You can feel her breath singeing your neck... Faster, faster...MOVE THOSE LEGS FOR CHRISTSAKES! *(on fire, moving in double time)* Now turn the other way to work against the current!

(Panting with exhaustion, they change direction. **MAGDA** *collapses and falls.)*

CANADA. *(rushing to* **MAGDA***)* STOP! STOP! WHAT DO YOU THINK YOU'RE DOING?

(The others freeze as **CANADA** *tends to* **MAGDA** *mumuring and checking her vital signs.)*

RO. *(crab walking and punching, yelling at the mythical starlet)* "This is *my* cab!," you yell. "You saw me hail it! What the fuck's the matter with you? You think just because you're the flavor of the month, I don't exist? You think youth runs the day?! Well, let me tell me you something, Missy. I'm an actor with ten times the craft you'll ever have! I go to my scene study class every day, work out at the gym, sleep four hours a night because I'm a nursing mother – and a single one at that – and I can *still* run the shit out of you! You wanna race for that cab? TRY AND CATCH ME, BITCH!"

*(***RO** *breaks into a crazy sprint, propelling herself forward with her weights as the others watch in horror.)*

JOAN. Ro, Ro, what are you doing?

APRIL. Stop it, stop it! You're going to drop dead!

CANADA. *(catching* **RO** *at the end of the lane, pinning her arms to her sides)* Easy, Ro, easy, I'm not going to hurt you. I just want you to stop running and calm down…

*(*RO *goes limp in her arms.)*

CANADA. Atta girl… *(taking her weights)* Relax…and let everything go… *(showing her)* Extend your arms as if you're a diva…some brilliant Italian diva being showered with bouquets after your tenth curtain call playing Musetta in "La Boheme." *(in an Italian accent, accepting her bouquets with an elegant swishing motion)* "Thank you… Thank you… *Grazie*… You're too kind… This means so much to me…" Echoes of your performance start to ring in your head…

("Musetta's Waltz" is heard in the distance, then gradually starts to swell.)

APRIL. Shhh…listen!

JOAN. I hear it! I hear it!

CANADA. *(sweeping the water, accepting her bouquets)* Thank you, thank you… *Grazie*…

ALL. *(joining her, accepting their bouquets)* "Thank you…thank you… *Grazie*…You're too kind…Why thank you. This means so much to me. Thank you, thank you…I'm so glad you enjoyed my performance.

MAGDA. *(back in her own language)* Thank you, thank you so much. You're too kind…

WHAT'S HER NAME. *(enters, stopping cold)* What's going on here?

APRIL. *(looking down)* Whoops, there goes my milk again… Look at it swirling between my fingers…It's like I'm melting into the pool…dissolving…milk and water becoming one I think I feel a poem coming on… *(accepting her bouquets)* "Thank you…thank you… *grazie* you're too kind…" *(etc. as…)*

CANADA. *(closing her eyes and swishing the water)* Now shut your eyes... That's it... Keep going...extend those arms...inhale those roses and lilies...The audience is going wild...*wild*! Just listen...

WHAT'S HER NAME. Ladies? *Ladies!*

APRIL. Shhh...

CANADA. It's alright, everything's under control.

APRIL. We're gathering our bouquets...and giving thanks.

> (*WHAT'S HER NAME watches in amazement as eyes closed, the class sweeps the water with rising brio, offering their thanks. The lights get very bright as "Musetta's Waltz" builds...and then quickly snaps out.*)

End of Play

Also by
Tina Howe...

Approaching Zanzibar
The Art of Dining
Birth and After Birth
Coastal Disturbances
Museum
One Shoe Off
Painting Churches
Pride's Crossing
Chasing Manet

Please visit our website **samuelfrench.com** for complete descriptions and licensing information

www.ingramcontent.com/pod-product-compliance
Lightning Source LLC
Chambersburg PA
CBHW070646300426
44111CB00013B/2289